Hello, My Name Is gets to the heart [...] homeless and the hero, the kid and th[...] diva—our identity. Matthew West no[...] presenting the powerful solution found only in Christ, but he has taken the time, literally hundreds of hours, to go to the grassroots to hear the stories of real people in their pursuit to escape the voices that lie to them and to grab hold of their adoption certificates as children of the one true King. This book will touch you deeply and threaten to change your life. And the song he wrote about it ain't half bad either.

—Randy Frazee
Senior Minister of Oak Hills Church,
author of *The Heart of the Story*

Matthew West brings the rare combination of songwriter and pastor to his ministry. He is a modern-day King David, creating Psalms that touch the heart of God and God's children. Now, as an added blessing to us all, he has compiled his thoughts into a book. A person can almost hear Matthew sing through the pages. I'm deeply grateful for this work, this singer, this friend.

—Max Lucado
New York Times best-selling author

This is a powerful book. Matthew is an inspiring storyteller who has the ability to tell other people's stories with empathy and grace. The gift inside these pages might just change the way you see yourself and help you live your own God-given story.

—Sheila Walsh
Author of *In the Middle of the Mess*

Hello, My Name Is will silence the lies of the enemy so you can hear God whisper, "You are mine. You are wanted. You are so incredibly loved."

—Lysa Terkeurst
New York Times best-selling author and
President of Proverbs 31 Ministries

Matthew West is one of those rare combinations of storyteller, songwriter, musician, vocalist, lyricist, lover of God and God's people. In *Hello, My Name Is,* he hits the mark inspiring us not to wear nametags that others give us but to embrace the names that come from our Father. Creative. Inspiring. Challenging. Everything Matthew West touches leaves a permanent mark on the soul. If you are ready to burst into your next assignment, this book is for you!

—Randy Phillips
Founder of Phillips, Craig & Dean
and Pastor of LifeAustin

Matthew's stories and experiences as a child, artist, husband, and father will make you laugh and cry as he conveys the message that finding true identity in this life cannot be found without a real and intimate relationship with Christ. Read this and discover it for yourself!

—Brian "Head" Welch
New York Times best-selling author of
Save Me from Myself and *With My Eyes Wide Open*

How we view ourselves is important. Understanding how God views us, though, makes a world of difference. Matthew West uses music and words—and now a book—to remind us of *Whose* we are so that once we embrace this truth, a new victory is ours to enjoy.

—Johnny Hunt
Pastor of First Baptist Church, Woodstock, GA

Matthew West is one of the good guys. He's a wonderful man, incredible husband/father, and a voice for all who need inspiration. Anytime he has something to say, I always listen.

—Scott Hamilton
Olympic gold medalist figure skater

Matthew West's engaging book *Hello, My Name Is* communicates the stories of life with the same powerful impact as his award-winning songs. Matthew uses humor, transparency, compelling storytelling, and biblical truths to inspire readers to live out their true identity. Living second to the things of God and serving others is not easy, but the journey he outlines offers a path to living authentically. Whether its songwriting, singing, or writing, Matthew is a true artist!

—I Am Second
iamsecond.com

This is a book that reads like a good talk with your best friend! That friend is Matthew West, who within these pages shares his journey, as well as others'. *Hello, My Name Is* encourages us to embrace the joy and freedom that comes with knowing who you are because you know WHOSE you are. The soundtrack to a new creation begins right here.

—Elisabeth Hasselbeck
"Child of the One True King,"
wife to Tim, and mom to Grace, Taylor, and Isaiah

Matthew West has always written honestly in his songs and stories. In his latest book, *Hello, My Name Is*, Matthew may offer his greatest truth yet: how to discover our God-given identity while building a closer relationship with our Lord. I gained a lot of insight while reading this book, and I know you will as well.

—Scotty McCreery
ACM, BMI, and CMT award-winning
country music entertainer and
author of *Go Big or Go Home: The Journey Toward the Dream*

HELLO MY NAME IS

Discover Your True Identity

MATTHEW WEST

WORTHY®
PUBLISHING

Published by Worthy Books, an imprint of Worthy Publishing Group, a division of Worthy Media, Inc., One Franklin Park, 6100 Tower Circle, Suite 210, Franklin, TN 37067.

WORTHY is a registered trademark of Worthy Media, Inc.

HELPING PEOPLE EXPERIENCE THE HEART OF GOD

eBook available wherever digital books are sold.
Audiobook available from Oasis Audio.

Names: West, Matthew, author.
Title: Hello, my name is... : discover your true identity / by Matthew West.
Description: Franklin, TN : Worthy Publishing, 2017.
Identifiers: LCCN 2017000686 | ISBN 9781617958601 (tradepaper)
Subjects: LCSH: Identity (Psychology)--Religious aspects--Christianity.
Classification: LCC BV4509.5 .W4333 2017 | DDC 248.4--dc23
LC record available at https://lccn.loc.gov/2017000686

For foreign and subsidiary rights, contact rights@worthypublishing.com

ISBN: 978-1-61795-860-1 (paperback)

17 18 19 20 21 LBM 8 7 6 5 4 3 2

To Emily, Lulu, and Delaney.
Hello, my name is "Thankful for You."

CONTENTS

WHAT'S ON YOUR NAMETAG?

I like to run. Not long distances. This body wasn't built for marathons. And not every day. Bad for the joints. And not when it's too hot outside. Honestly, who wants to sweat that much? And don't get me started on the chafing. Oh, and I can't run in chilly weather either. Wouldn't want to catch a cold . . .

Come to think of it, I'm not sure I actually like running after all.

Perhaps it's just the *idea* of running that I am so fond of. When that one perfect day comes along (every six months or so), boy does it feel good to lace up the old sneakers and go out exploring! And that's what I love best about going for a jog. Running provides a rare opportunity to witness the world around me for at least a few minutes without being plugged in to some sort of mobile device that is competing for my attention. It never fails that as I run, somehow God seems to open my eyes and show me something new. That's what happened last weekend.

The stars aligned, and that perfect day to run had arrived. I was traveling through a new city and was excited to explore the area a bit. As I exited my hotel, I found a trail that ran along a river and decided *that* would be my path. I was not even ten minutes into my run when I passed a park bench occupied by a homeless man. It was clear that this uncomfortable-looking, metal-framed stopping post had served as his bed for the night, or at least for the last several hours. And although it was broad daylight, he was still passed out, showing no signs of waking. In the few seconds it took me to jog past him, I was struck by three distinct snapshots that I still can't get out of my head.

First, he had a young face. Although he had one arm covering his eyes to shield the sun, I could tell this man was probably in his early thirties, maybe around my age. Second, on his wrist I noticed a rubber bracelet with the words "Aim High" painted in white across it. But the most peculiar part of this heartbreaking picture was the book he clutched to his chest with his other arm the way a little child hugs her teddy bear while sleeping. Not wanting to stop and risk waking him, I continued running down the path, but all the while wondering what book he was clinging to so tightly as he slept.

Much to my appreciation, the trail came to an end about a mile down the river, and I had no choice but to head back the way I came and hopefully hang up my running shoes for another six months. As I ran back, I wondered if that guy on the bench would still be sleeping when I passed him again. My pace quickened as I thought of that book he was holding. Within minutes, I saw that this young man had yet to move, but now I could make out some of the words on the cover as I passed by: "Class of 2001." It was a high school yearbook.

I imagined that was his yearbook. I imagined it held inside a picture of a younger, more hopeful version of the man who was out cold on that park bench by the river. I imagined the inside cover was filled with messages from former friends exchanging best wishes on graduation day. Things like, "Hey, buddy! Have a great summer. Stay cool!" Or maybe a message from a girl he had a crush on that said, "Call me this summer," along with her phone number inside the shape of a heart. I imagined pages featuring "Most Likely" awards, where he may have been voted "Most likely to succeed" or "Most likely to find a cure for cancer." Ultimately, I imagined that maybe, just maybe, he was holding on to that book so he could remember a time filled with . . .

More promise, less failure.
More good times, less mistakes.
More opportunities, less regrets.
More future, less past.

Maybe you, too, are trying to remember a more promising time in your life. Maybe you are not sure you like where you've been or who you've become. Maybe you're struggling to find your true identity or how exactly you fit into this crazy world. Maybe someone has made you believe a lie about who you are by speaking damaging words to you. Well, you're not alone. Every single one of us has a difficult journey to discover our true, God-given identity. E. E. Cummings wrote,

To be nobody but yourself in a world which is doing its best, night and day, to make you just like everybody else means to fight the hardest battle any human being can fight; and never stop fighting.

HELLO, MY NAME IS JORDAN

The story I received from a young man named Jordan so powerfully illustrated this "fight" for identity Mr. Cummings referenced that he inspired the song that, in turn, inspired this book you are holding. The very first sentence of Jordan's letter to me read, "Hello, my name is Jordan and I'm a drug addict." Jordan went on to tell me his story of growing up as a preacher's kid in a small Tennessee town. He was always the "good" kid, never got into any trouble. Jordan was a gifted athlete. He could run. Fast. We're talking Forrest Gump fast. He received an athletic scholarship and became a seven-time all-American in track and field. But during his sophomore season Jordan badly broke his ankle. That was when he received his first prescription for the pain medication OxyContin. Jordan said he felt like he'd lost his identity as the big man on campus and the star athlete, and he began to find his identity in that pain medication as addiction began to take over his life. After two failed drug tests, Jordan hit rock bottom. He was kicked out of college, stripped of his scholarship and his beloved sports. Because his parents begged him to get help and not let his addiction have the last say in his life, Jordan agreed to enter a yearlong Christian recovery program called Teen Challenge.

During his time in Teen Challenge, Jordan began to realize that all his life he had been seeking and finding his identity in the wrong things. Oh, they weren't all bad things on the surface. But that's just it, they were *on the surface*. "Preacher's son." "Good kid." "Star athlete." Jordan thought those titles defined him. It wasn't until bad choices were made and some of those identities he was so proud of were wiped away that he realized his true identity was waiting to be discovered *beneath* the surface. Now he was being tempted to try on some different names for size. Names like "Addict," "Failure," and "Regret."

But as Jordan spent his time in recovery praying and reading his Bible, God did a powerful work in his life. God began showing him that he isn't defined by his successes *or* his failures but that his true identity is found in the one who made him and loves him deeply. "Therefore, if anyone is in Christ, he is a new creation; old things have passed away; behold, all things have become new" (2 Corinthians 5:17 NKJV). Someone once said, "Let your only evaluation of worth derive from the awareness of God's love for you. All other measures leave one in a state of delusion."

Jordan decided to embrace his new identity in Christ, and that was the key to the miraculous transformation in his life. He graduated from recovery after a year, but he knew that he had some more graduating to do. He went back to the same college that kicked him out and earned his master's degree! They even allowed him to run for the track and field team one more time. (I bet he could give me a few pointers on the whole running thing.) Today, Jordan is a high school teacher and varsity basketball coach. God has blessed him with a beautiful wife and has radically restored Jordan's relationships with family and friends. The last sentence of the story Jordan wrote to me said, "I no longer introduce myself as an addict. Instead I can say, 'Hello, my name is Jordan and I am a child of the One True King!'"

DISCOVERING WHO YOU ARE

You do have a nametag, you know. It is as if the doctor slapped a nametag right on the outside of your first onesie in the delivery room and, with a push out the door, shouted, "Welcome to the world, go make a name for yourself." Of course, we are each given a birth name, one decided on by our parents. And while that name may carry some meaning or family significance, that's not the name I'm talking about. No, we are thirsty for real meaning, waiting for something more. Our birth name does not hold the answer to the questions we ask ourselves, does not fill in the blank at the end of "Hello, my name is _____." From my earliest memories of childhood, I've been trying to fill in that blank, living as though it's up to me to tell the world I'm significant.

Throughout our lives, we all try on different nametags and identities, seeing what fits, what feels right, what seems to be accepted or liked by the people around us. We choose names that make us feel good, proud, distinguished. Unfortunately, some names find their way on our nametags as a result of failures and regrets. Still others are given to us by outside influences—names that hurt us and negatively affect our view of who we are. Over time our nametags can get pretty crowded, and while some of the names on our nametags might be accurate in describing one facet or another of our lives, those names fail to capture our full identity. They may describe the outer layers, but they don't come close to the core of who we are. Those names may represent the bullet points, mere chapters of our lives, but they could never accurately title the story of our lives. The more we start to own or accept those names, the further we may find ourselves from our true identity.

Just as Satan deceived Adam and Eve in the garden, he would love for nothing more than to get you to believe lies about yourself. He knows that if you take ownership of a false identity, before long that identity will own *you*. And the more time you spend being owned by a false identity, the further away you fall from discovering and tapping into the power and the freedom and the hope found in the truth of who God says you are. That is the key: you can't discover who you are until you first acknowledge *whose* you are.

What if I told you it wasn't up to you to fill in that blank? What if I told you those negative identities that have landed on your nametags don't have to stay there? My prayer is that this book might serve as a wake-up call for you to take a good look at your nametag. This book will challenge you to get honest with yourself. Most of all, I pray you will be overwhelmed by the powerful promise that those old names don't have to own you anymore. After all, only God writes your name with permanent marker—all other names can be erased.

Just like Jordan, your true identity has already been given to you, and it's the only title that really matters. You are a CHILD OF THE ONE TRUE KING!

> *See what great love the father has lavished on us,*
> *that we should be called children of God!*
> *And that is what we are! (1 John 3:1)*

THE
GREATEST
TRUTH

Understanding Who You Are Starts
with Knowing Whose You Are

CHAPTER 1

MY NEW BEST FRIEND

"Are we going to be friends forever?" asked Piglet.
"Even longer," Pooh answered.

A. A. MILNE

She was all dressed up in a brand-new outfit from head to toe. Color-coordinated, of course. Lulu was born with an eye for fashion just like her momma. Her favorite color? Well, one look at family photo albums or her bedroom décor and you'd find the answer in no time: PINK! Two pink bows holding pigtails in place. Pink shoelaces laced up her new, predominantly pink sneakers, which were filled by unbearably cute little feet wearing frilly pink socks. Those socks paired perfectly with her brand-new backpack. Can you guess what color? Yep.

Now, for a guy who grew up pretending to be Hulk Hogan, practicing pro wrestling moves with two brothers in the backyard, this new world of tutus, tiaras, and the color pink frightened and confused me at first. I have learned the hard way that a father of two girls has as much of a chance escaping the house on a given day without his fingernails painted a bright shade of fuchsia as my little brother had escaping one of my backyard body slams. Reaching for my coffee cup at Starbucks and noticing the hipster barista staring at my painted nails prompts nothing but a grin and one word: "Daughters."

Well, the time had come. Lulu, my five-year-old fashionista, was ready to make a splash on her first day of school. And this was not just any first day of school. This was *the* first day of school. As in, the first *ever* day of school. The big dance. The show. Kindergarten! My little pink princess was poised and ready to venture out into the great academic unknown, her long, yellow chariot awaiting her. For her mother and me, the closing of the bus door and the folding of that stop sign signified the start of our countdown.

Time sure took its own sweet time that day. As we awaited Lulu's return from her first day of kindergarten, questions grew thick around us. Did she remember to eat her lunch? Was she scared in her new classroom? Had she made any friends? Were the other kids nice to her? I remember how we walked to the bus stop a good twenty minutes early that afternoon, homemade posterboard signs in hand that read "Congratulations, Genius!" Now, I'm not sure what changed, but she got on that bus my little baby girl . . . and when she stepped off hours later, she looked like Little Miss Independent as she tossed her backpack into my arms and began skipping down the sidewalk toward home. As her mother and I ran to catch up with her, a little game of Twenty Questions ensued.

"Lulu, tell us all about it! How was your first day?"

"It was great!" she replied with a toothless grin. "I made a new best friend!"

"That's great, Lulu! What's your new best friend's name?"

She stopped for a second, rolled her eyes up as if she were trying to see the top of her head, and then with a shrug answered, "I don't know. But she's my best friend!"

MY BEST FRIEND'S NAME

I have a best friend too. One who knows me better than anyone does. One who has never left me. One who loves me deeply. My best friend carries me through my most difficult days. I talk about my best friend often. I even write books and compose and record songs proclaiming how much I love my best friend and how much he loves me. Yes, like Lulu after her first day of kindergarten, I can shout, "I've got a best friend!"

I grew up fascinated by Sunday school stories about this man named Jesus. How he spread mud on the eyes of a blind man and gave him sight (John 9). How he fed more than five thousand hungry people from just five loaves of bread and a couple of fish (Matthew 14). How he brought his friend Lazarus back from the dead (John 11). How he sacrificed his own life, an innocent man being put to death (Luke 23). How he rose from the dead three days later (Luke 24). I remember feeling an undeniable stirring in my soul when I first read scriptures describing the power of Jesus's name. "Therefore God has highly exalted him and bestowed on him the name that is above every name, so that at the name of Jesus every knee should bow, in heaven and on earth and under the earth, and every tongue confess that Jesus Christ is Lord, to the glory of God the Father" (Philippians 2:9–11 ESV). But what really blew me away was learning that this powerful, miracle-working, life-sacrificing Jesus calls *me* friend. "I no longer call you servants . . . Instead, I have called you friends" (John 15:15 NIV). On Sunday mornings, I would stand with my family and sing timeless hymns that told me so.

> *What a friend we have in Jesus*
> *All our sins and griefs to bear*
> *What a privilege to carry*
> *Everything to God in prayer*

I wanted to know this Jesus. I had read, "Everyone who calls on the name of the Lord will be saved" (Romans 10:13 NIV), so at the age of thirteen I prayed. I talked to Jesus and asked him into my heart while watching a televised Billy Graham crusade. That began my journey with my new best friend.

Yet, if I'm being honest, I'm afraid I would lose count of how many times I live my life as if I've forgotten my best friend's name and the power that name holds. The years since that first prayer have at times forced a forgetfulness that mirrors Lulu's return from her first day of kindergarten. Somewhere between the playground and the bus ride home, she forgot the name of her new best friend. Somewhere between a bedtime prayer of a junior high kid and a Monday-morning crisis in the real world of an adult, I have done the same.

WHAT'S MY NAME AGAIN?

Can you remember how *you* felt on your first day of school? Remember walking into a new classroom for the first time? Even as I write this, I'm having flashbacks of my own kindergarten initiation, and it's making me start to perspire. I was so nervous that I could hardly remember my *own* name, let alone the name of a new friend I might have just met. Come to think of it, the first day of kindergarten (and every day since) has been a challenge to do two things: (1) Remember who I am and (2) Remember who my best friend is.

Oscar Wilde wrote, "Most people are other people. Their thoughts are someone else's opinions, their lives a mimicry, their passions a quotation." Sadly, I'm afraid there are times when we live that way. Perhaps this is because the journey that leads us to the core of who we really are requires a level of honesty that makes us feel uncomfortable. Oh, but we were born for that journey! And deep down, we crave the freedom that is hidden behind the honesty it takes to find it. Not one of us aspires to be a replica, because we were never created to be a copy. Not Lulu the kindergartner. Not me. Not you. Even identical twins each have unique fingerprint patterns. And you were meant to leave your one-of-a-kind fingerprint on this life, this world. No one knows this better than our Creator. After all, each of us is his idea. And his idea to create you comes with a perfect plan. "For I know the plans I have for you . . . plans for good and not for disaster, to give you a future and a hope" (Jeremiah 29:11).

Don't know who you are? God does. Don't have a plan for your life? God does. Don't see any hope? God does. Don't see anything but disaster? God does. Discovering our true identities does not begin by looking within ourselves, but by looking *outside* of ourselves to the one who made us. There is no greater authority on your life than the one who gave you life. The more you get to know him, the more you will discover who he created you to be.

These days Lulu is a book-reading, sentence-writing, number-adding, piano-playing, dance-class-taking fourth grader. I am happy to announce that she did eventually remember the name of the best friend she made on her first day of kindergarten, and as I am writing this chapter, I can hear them upstairs playing. Lulu is learning who she is. And she remembered who her best friend is. Do you remember who yours is?

If Jesus is your best friend, how is it possible to forget his name and the power in that name?

When do you forget who you are and end up living someone else's life, rather than the one God has for you?

Read Jeremiah 29:11. God says that he has great plans for you. How can you live in such a way that shows you believe that promise? When do you struggle to believe it?

CHAPTER 2

OOH, THAT'S
MY FAVORITE!

If you can't see the sun you will be impressed with a street light.
If you've never felt thunder and lightning
you'll be impressed with fireworks.

JOHN PIPER

You don't want to watch fireworks on the Fourth of July with me. I'm quite annoying. At least that's what my family tells me. And I'm sure they tell me that in love. It's like when someone begins a sentence by saying, "No offense, but . . . ," chances are they are about to offend you. But I can't really blame them. I am *that* guy. The annoying one who can't keep quiet during our town's pyrotechnic display of patriotism. The guy who tries to get my family to say "ooooh" after one firework and "ahhhh" after the next. For some reason, they never join in.

I also like to name the fireworks based on their unique characteristics. Let's see, there's the "Weeping Willow," which is the sparkly one that looks like it's raining down over the crowd. There's the "Dipsy-Doodle" that spins off like little spirals in the sky. There's also the "Silent but Deadly," "Merry Christmas," "Swirly-Twirly Gumdrop," "Smiley Face" . . . Well, you get the idea. Hey, I'm a songwriter. I name things. It's what I do.

As if that's not annoying enough, the final and perhaps most obnoxious thing I like to do after every "ooh" and "ahh" is to shout, "That's my favorite!" Then, when the next firework explodes, my family will hear me say, "No, I just changed my mind. *That's* my favorite!" By the end of each fireworks show, I have proudly declared that every blast was better than the last and each one my favorite. Hey, that may be annoying, but it could be worse. I could dress up like Larry the Cable Guy every Fourth of July, wearing a T-shirt with a giant bald eagle spray-painted on the front and the sleeves cut off as I launch roman candles from my driveway while hollering, "'Merica!" That's the power of perspective, people.

HELLO, MY NAME IS "AMAZED"

As I began researching for this book, I found myself echoing the same refrain after discovering each of the names given to God throughout Scripture. "Ooh, that's my favorite!" Every name reveals a different dimension of the awesomeness and wonder of the God I thought I already knew. Digging deeper opened my eyes to see that for too long I had settled for a surface knowledge and understanding of who God is, all the while spending much more time focusing on figuring out who I am. I confess that before I engaged in this exercise of studying and meditating on who God is, I had handled the power of his name with about as little reverence as the catchy childhood premeal prayer, "God is great. God is good. Thank you, God, for this food. Amen." Perhaps you know what I'm talking about. We begin a prayer by saying, "Dear God" or "Heavenly Father," but have we truly explored the great depth of who he is? We may even know some of his other names, but are they mere words with no meaning to us? Or worse?

Recently I was exiting a plane after a flight from Los Angeles to Nashville. Still somewhat groggy from my four-and-a-half-hour journey, I slowly made the brief trek up the walkway into the airport. As I did, a middle-aged woman in front of me accidentally dropped her bag. As she bent down to retrieve her luggage, she shouted in frustration, "Jesus Christ!" This stopped me in my tracks as I was reminded of the reality that for some, God's name is nothing but a swear word, something shouted out of anger as a curse rather than something spoken in adoration as praise. For many, the name of God has been reduced to nothing more than slang used in everyday conversation. "Oh my God! Look at these shoes!" You get the idea. And perhaps this is something you find yourself doing as well.

I once heard Rick Warren say the very fact that people use the name of God as a curse word is proof that we all have an internal leaning in the direction of one who is greater than us. Think about it. When that woman dropped her bag in the airport, she didn't shout, "Oh Matthew West!" or "Oh my spouse!" She didn't curse another human being. Even in her cursing, she was unconsciously acknowledging that there is something different, something greater, about the name of Jesus.

The angel Gabriel didn't mince words. Perhaps that's why God gave this trusty celestial sidekick so many assignments. When he appeared to Mary to tell her the news that her world was about to be totally turned upside down because she had been chosen to carry the long-awaited Savior of the world, Gabriel left nothing to chance. "You will conceive and give birth to a son, and you will name him Jesus. He will be very great and will be called the Son of the Most High" (Luke 1:31–32). Gabriel's first order of business? Telling Mary what to expect while she was expecting. His second assignment? Making sure she didn't worry about picking a name. His name had already been decided: Jesus. The name means "Savior." An angel also appeared to Joseph, Mary's troubled fiancé, who had just found out his bride-to-be was already a mother-to-be. To Joseph, the instructions to name the baby Jesus were followed by a reason: "She will give birth to a son, and you are to give him the name Jesus, because he will save his people from their sins" (Matthew 1:21 NIV).

THERE'S A NAME FOR THAT

Shakespeare famously posed the question, "What's in a name?" "That which we call a rose by any other word would smell as sweet." The giver of all names answered that very question long before he even breathed life into Shakespeare's lungs. Not all names are equal. There *is* one name above all others. "Therefore God exalted him to the highest place and gave him the name that is above every name" (Philippians 2:9 NIV). His name had been chosen long before heaven's chosen was born in Bethlehem. That's how significant the name of Jesus is. New Testament Scripture even points back to Old Testament prophecies that foretold the name of our Savior long before his arrival. The Bible shows us that everything taking place was fulfilling what "the Lord had said through the prophet: 'The virgin will conceive and give birth to a son, and they will call him Immanuel' (which means 'God with us')" (Matthew 1:22–23 NIV).

Isaiah gave us an even longer list of some of the many names that would add up to describe the splendor of our Savior. "And he will be called: Wonderful Counselor, Mighty God, Everlasting Father, Prince of Peace" (Isaiah 9:6). Yes, throughout Scripture Jesus is given many names, and they all ring true in our daily lives. But why didn't the Bible just stop at the name Jesus? Wouldn't it be enough to know that in him we have a Savior? It's as if God went to great lengths not only to tell us we have a Savior but to *show* us all of the different ways he can and will save us from ourselves. Each name speaks to specific needs we have in our lives. The smartphone craze has created a world of applications (or "apps") that provide any number of functions—from video games to financial planning to photography tools. Apple even trademarked the slogan "There's an app for that." When it comes to the names of our Savior, the same is true. Got a need? There's a name for that . . .

Your name may be "Confused" . . .
His name is *Wonderful Counselor* (Isaiah 9:6).

Your name may be "Lonely" . . .
His name is *Immanuel* (Matthew 1:23).

Your name may be "Lost" . . .
His name is *Good Shepherd* (John 10:11).

Your name may be "Failure" . . .
His name is *Redeemer* (Job 19:25).

Your name may be "Desperate" . . .
His name is *Jehovah Jireh,* or *God Will Provide* (Genesis 22:14).

Your name may be "Troubled" . . .
His name is *Prince of Peace* (Isaiah 9:6).

Your name may be "Weak" . . .
His name is *Mighty God* (Isaiah 9:6).

Your name may be "Broken" . . .
His name is *Healer* (Exodus 15:26).

Every negative or false identity is a sign of something we lack, something we need, a problem we can't solve on our own. It cannot be mere coincidence that each of these names given to God is a promise that he will fill every void, provide every need, and solve every problem. Not only are the names of God an indication of who he is, but they are also an invitation for us to come to him just as we are.

DON'T TROUBLE THE TEACHER

Did you know the phrase *aha moment* is actually in the dictionary? Evidently, this is largely credited to Oprah's use of it, so I guess we have her to thank for the ability to voice our moments of sudden realization. I had many aha moments while reading and studying the various names of God, and each time this thought hit me: *Would Scripture highlight all of God's amazing attributes only to dissuade me from coming into his presence?* I sure don't think so. Instead, with every discovery about God through each of his names, we are invited into his presence to find that which we need. All the false names we put on or allow others to force on us expose our deepest failures, insecurities, and needs that only he can fulfill. His names point us back to the one who knows our needs even before we do (Matthew 6:8), and he supplies all of them (Philippians 4:19).

Even with this knowledge, have you ever kept yourself from bringing a particular prayer request to God? I know I have. I notice this happening in my thought process from time to time. I tend to prioritize my prayer needs as if I believe God does the same when we come to him. Instead of going to God with *everything* that is on my heart, or every false identity that I'm struggling with, I tend to decide for myself what is worthy of his attention. Here are some thoughts that enter my mind in those times:

There are people in the world with much bigger problems today than what I am facing.

I should only go to God with the big stuff. I don't want to trouble him with every little thing.

My situation is too far beyond repair. It must be God's will for it to end this way, so why bother?

The problem I'm having now is a result of me not following God's plan in the first place. I'm just going to have to see this one through on my own.

Do any of these thoughts resonate with you? Perhaps you've found yourself thinking the same thing, and as a result you have edited your prayers to present to God a more "appropriate" request. Although I allow these thoughts to enter into my mind occasionally, do I believe they are true? No. I know the truth. And I'm sure you do too. It's just that with all of the emphasis the Bible places on the importance of prayer, it should be no wonder that the Devil uses whatever tactics he can to steer us away from having open, honest dialogue with our Creator.

I struggle with the same "editing" process when I'm writing songs. For a long time I would put unnecessary pressure on myself to have the first draft of my lyrics be the final draft, as if the very first words to appear on the page were supposed to be pure poetry and perfectly written. I don't know, maybe I just wanted to be able to tell VH1 when they come to film my

"Behind the Music" story how it was just a magical moment of inspiration. And while there may be moments of inspiration when the pen hits the paper and the right words just seem to flow immediately, they are just that—moments. Moments in the midst of hours, days, sometimes weeks of working at it, pouring words out until it feels right. If a songwriter begins editing the song right out of the gate, there is a good chance that song will never be heard, because chances are it will never be written. Only in the last few years have I begun to embrace the freedom of simply pouring out my words on a page and not worrying about editing them or trying to make them perfect right away. In doing this, I'm able to find my way to the heart of the matter, because I'm letting my heart sort through all that it is feeling and desiring to communicate. Many times this process results in discovering something completely different from what I was supposed to write about that day.

What if we took this same approach when we pray? No more editing. No more sorting. No more deciding for God what he needs to be troubled with. After all, God has a much better handle on our hearts' desires than we often acknowledge, and he "knows exactly what you need even before you ask him" (Matthew 6:8). He also invites us to bring every one of those needs to Him, no editing. "Give *all* your worries and cares to God, for he cares about you" (1 Peter 5:7, emphasis mine). In the book of Luke, a man named Jairus fell at Jesus's feet and begged him to come to his home because his twelve-year-old daughter was dying. Jesus was on his way to the little girl when a messenger approached Jairus with a discouraging update. He told Jairus, "Your daughter is dead. There's no use troubling the Teacher now" (8:49). But Jesus said to Jairus, "Don't be afraid. Just have faith, and she will be healed" (v. 50). Jesus was saying to Jairus, "It's no trouble at all. I know your need, and I'm glad you came to me with it." Instead of Jairus saying, "Well, Jesus, never mind. Don't bother coming to my home now," he ignored the messenger and obeyed the Savior. As a result, his daughter was healed.

Satan acts like the messenger in our lives, saying, "Don't trouble the teacher with that request" or "Do you honestly think God has time for your little problems?" or "That part of your story is way too messy. I wouldn't dare show that to God." Jesus says, "Don't listen to that messenger. Bring it all to me, and I will show you that I have all you need."

THE BOY WHO DANCED

Ian caught my attention from the moment I walked on stage. A little guy about six years old, he must have had the entire contents of his mom's bottle of Aqua Net hair spray holding his hair in place to look like a little Mohawk. Yep, Ian was ready for the big concert. But here's why this boy really caught my eye. From the first note of the first song we played until the final note of the last song, Ian danced. He danced harder with each new song we played as if to say, "Ooh, *that's* my favorite." And his dancing wasn't a polite, swaying back and forth, church-crowd kind of dancing. No way. Ian was jumping and sliding and pumping his fists in the air. He did the moon walk, the running man, even some kind of break-dancing. You know how they say, "Dance like no one's watching"? Well, Ian was following those instructions to a T. It was as if Ian wouldn't have been able to stop dancing if he tried.

I noticed that every few seconds he would look down at his shoes, and I quickly realized why. Ian was wearing the kind of sneakers that light up upon movement. *Dancing with the Stars* had nothing on this kid. Not only was he a dancing fool, he was a walking light show! I was so captivated by this joy-filled little boy that I forgot the words to the song I was singing. So I decided there was one thing for me to do—invite Ian to bring his show on my stage so that my audience could be as entertained as I was. What happened next was a hilariously fantastic display of happy feet. As I started strumming my guitar, the crowd stood and began clapping their hands in rhythm. And Ian? Well, Ian made the stage his dance floor, and the crowd's eyes lit up right along with his shoes. With every step and every slide, the crowd just laughed and cheered for the little boy who stole the show with his glow-in-the-dark shoes and joyful heart.

I want that kind of joy. Don't you? The kind that makes you break into a dance no matter how crazy you look. Imagine the joy that must have filled Jairus and his family when they watched Jesus bring their beloved little girl back to life! I bet Jairus sure was glad that he troubled the Teacher that day. I imagine he and his family might've put on their dancing sandals and broken into some kind of a New Testament electric slide! Jairus's daughter was alive, freed from the grips of death that held her moments before. And with freedom comes joy. The kind of joy that makes you want to dance. The kind of joy you can't even explain. The kind the Bible describes as "an inexpressible and glorious joy" (1 Peter 1:8 NIV).

There is freedom in the realization that each name given to our Savior is a divine invitation given to us. A call to come to him as Jairus did, with faith that he can and will work a miracle. With that freedom comes great and *inexpressible* joy. Joy because the "name above all other names" helps us discover our true name (Philippians 2:9). Joy because we don't have to listen to the messenger who discourages us from troubling the teacher. Joy because for everything we lack, our Savior provides.

Now, if you'll excuse me, it's time for me to dust off my dancing shoes.

How amazed are you at God and who he is? Or do you tune him out from time to time, treating him as "same old same old"?

Looking at the names of God listed in this chapter (Wonderful Counselor, Redeemer, Prince of Peace, and others), which of them have impacted you at different times?

Read 1 Peter 1:8. When have you felt "an inexpressible and glorious joy" that makes you want to dance? What's keeping you from dancing now?

CHAPTER 3

BIRD POOP
AND OTHER THINGS
I NEVER SAW COMING

A bird in the hand . . .
probably means poop in the hand soon.

ME

Birds hate me. I am convinced of this. I'm pretty sure the hatred actually extends to my whole family. For a long time I did not know the reason why. I couldn't remember ever doing anything to provoke them. Is it because we cook a Thanksgiving turkey each year? Can't be. Everyone does that. Is it because I went quail hunting once? There's no way. I'm a horrible shot. Perhaps it was some relative from years ago that made birds decide the West family would forever be on their hit list. You know, like Jaws 1, 2, 3, 4, 5, 6, and 7. (How many were there?) In search for a reason why birds seem to harbor such bitterness toward me, I began an investigation to uncover the genesis of our family feud with these feathered creatures.

Turns out, my sweet mother once had a pet parakeet named Cheerio when she was a child. Cheerio was blind. Yes, you read that right. My mother had a blind bird named Cheerio. You can't make this stuff up, people. And for some reason, my grandmother occasionally allowed my mother to let Cheerio out of its cage to fly around the house. Ever seen a blind bird fly? Well, my mom said it wasn't pretty. Evidently, the takeoff was never the problem. It was the landing that Cheerio couldn't quite stick . . . or maybe stuck too often and too abruptly. That poor bird would just fly back and forth slamming into one wall after another and sliding down to the floor. I imagine a little circle of cartoon stars around its dizzy little head until Cheerio would take off again, hoping that one of these days he'd get lucky enough to find a wall with an open window. But that never happened. Poor Cheerio.

I now believe this to be overwhelming evidence that points to the reason why birds have been out to get me for all these years. Here is my theory: Cheerio must have harbored great hatred toward my mother for allowing it to fly into so many walls. And I bet those birds can really get to talking. Yep, word spreads fast among the fowl. Why else do you think they're always chirping? To this day, they use my car for target practice. I'm pretty sure they follow me, because how else would they know when I get a car wash? I could be sitting by the lake enjoying a nice spring afternoon with my daughter and those ducks would chase me down as if I were a homemade loaf of white bread. I could be soaking up the sun at my favorite beach when out of nowhere those seagulls dive-bomb my beach chair as though it were covered in she-crab.

Not long ago, I was taking a walk in a new city to explore the sights. I lost track of time and also of my location, so I stopped to consult my trusty smartphone, seeking directions back to my hotel. Standing on a street corner and staring down at my phone, I heard what sounded like a pigeon cooing overhead. I looked up to find public enemy number one squaring off for a little target practice from the top of a street light. And . . . bull's-eye! That bird pooped right on my head. I should have seen it coming. Now, in my moment of anger, I might not have seen things clearly, but I could have sworn I saw that bird smile as it took flight, surely headed to torture another one of my family members. And as it flew off, I am pretty sure I heard the pigeon speak to me in a New York accent, "That one's for Cheerio!" I like to think all pigeons have New York accents. Maybe there's even a pigeon mafia. Anyway, score another one for the birds. And thanks a lot, Mom.

HELLO, MY NAME IS "CONTROL FREAK"

A sneak attack from a vengeful pigeon with pinpoint accuracy isn't the only unexpected occurrence that catches me by surprise on a given day. In fact, rare is the day that goes exactly the way I have planned. I'm imagining you nodding your head in agreement with me. But here's my problem with this: I'm what you might call a control freak. I'm allergic to unwanted detours. I want to go where I want to go and arrive when I plan to arrive. When I'm there, wherever "there" is, I expect things to go exactly the way I had imagined. I know there is no such thing as a perfect day, but I want mine to be as close to perfect as possible.

This part of my personality drives my wife absolutely nuts on date nights and vacations. Especially vacations. I get this picture in my head of how picture-perfect our family beach trip should be, and if even the slightest interruption occurs, it can throw me into a funk. Did you know the beach is the worst place for a control freak to travel? On the coast, the locals echo old Mark Twain with the saying, "If you don't like the weather here, just wait a few minutes." In the days leading up to our summer beach vacation, the control freak in me makes the fatal error of grabbing my iPhone and asking Siri to check, recheck, and then triple-check the weather forecast for the particular area where we will be heading. I can picture the dream-shattering image on my iPhone now—that little cloud icon with the lightning bolt cutting through it. And it's never forecast for an occasional day or two, but for EVERY SINGLE DAY of our scheduled vacation. That's when the panic begins.

"Honey, do you think we should cancel our trip?"

"No, Matthew. It will be fine. It always is," my wife assures me with a roll of her eyes.

"But, but, but there's a tropical disturbance in the middle of the ocean that just may turn into a tropical storm with a girl's name, which has a five percent chance of turning into a hurricane that could arrive the second night we are down there. This has the potential to become quite a storm! You see that little lightning bolt in the cloud icon?"

"Take a deep breath, honey. It's going to be fine." And guess what? She's right. It always turns out okay. Sure, there might be the occasional rainy day when we'd rather be out soaking up the sun. But I inevitably discover (or actually *re*discover) that my family and I have the time of our lives regardless of the weather. In fact, some of our most memorable times wind up being the previously dreaded rainy days that Siri warned us about. On those days, our swimsuits stay dry as we huddle around the table with each other and enjoy the many complexities of Monopoly. Control freaks are slow learners.

The more I think about it, unexpected changes of plans are not always bad. It's just the not knowing that drives control freaks like me crazy. That's why there is one thing I envy about birds. Did you know some birds' vision can be up to eight times stronger than the average human's? An eagle can spot its prey from a mile away. As much as those feathered enemies of mine frustrate me, I do wish I could see the world from a bird's-eye view every once in a while. Don't you? If I had my way, things would always go . . . well, *my* way. But we all know that life brings about unwanted interruptions, challenges, and even trials.

Wouldn't it be great to fly high above it all and get an accurate view of what's up ahead? That way nothing would ever catch us off guard. Instead of getting blindsided with a pink slip at work one Friday, you could see it coming months in advance and have a head start looking for a job. You could see that your child is going to struggle in his math studies when he hits fifth grade, so you set him up with a tutor long before then. With a bird's-eye view, the "un" would be erased from *unexpected* and we could plan accordingly.

I have a friend who has spent the last several years as a meteorologist, studying and reporting the weather on a major local news station in the city where I live. He told me that he's always had a passion for the weather. Ever since he was a child, he would watch the clouds and dream of becoming a meteorologist. Over dinner one night, I jokingly asked him if people ever get mad at him when the weather forecast winds up being wrong. He said, "Boy, do they ever!" and then proceeded to tell me stories of the hate mail he has received. "Dear Weatherman, how dare you predict sunny with a high of seventy-five! It rained the entire day of my daughter's wedding, and I blame YOU!" "Dear Weatherman, you wouldn't know a sunny day if it hit you in the face!" "Dear Weatherman, I hope a bird poops on your car!" (That one was actually from me after it rained during my vacation.) He even said there had been times when people noticed him out on the street on a day that had shaped up to be different from his forecast, and they would point to the sky with a frustrated look on their face as if to say, "Nice going. You really nailed this one."

Funny thing about my meteorologist friend: he's now in the real estate business. Recently, I asked him if he missed reporting the weather. His response was unintentionally profound. "You know, I don't miss it like I thought I would. For a long time I was studying the weather because it was my job, but now I love it again like I used to as a kid. I get a kick out of going out in the fields and seeing those storm clouds roll in. These days I just enjoy watching the weather change." You might be wondering what I was wondering. Who on earth enjoys watching the weather change? Evidently only a former weatherman. Certainly not a beach-going control freak like me. But my friend's unique take on the changing weather got me thinking. It was no longer his job to predict whether or not the weather would change. (See what I did there? Not impressed? Okay. Moving on.) It wasn't up to him to decide if people should stay inside because a snowstorm was approaching or if a family should grab their swimsuits and head to the beach. He was off the hook.

I've got great news: you and I are off the hook too. It's not our responsibility to predict or control the changes in our daily circumstances. Never has been. The one who decides where lightning will strike and how much rain will fall is the same one who controls your life and this changing world in which we live. Forget a bird's-eye view. Ain't a bird around that can fly high enough to see all that God sees. He is the only one with a *God's-eye view*. Not the birds. Not me. And not you. "For just as the heavens are higher than the earth, so my ways are higher than your ways and my thoughts higher than your thoughts" (Isaiah 55:9). This means that those things that catch us off guard are never a surprise to God. His knowledge is limitless. He is aware of all things at all times. His "understanding is infinite" (Psalm 147:5 NKJV). When life is derailed by an unexpected detour, God is not looking down from heaven thinking, *Woah, I did NOT see that coming!* What a comforting thought that is.

If we acknowledge God as all-knowing and in control, we must at the same time acknowledge that we are none of those things. We can't have it both ways. I can't say, "God, I trust you," and then turn around and frantically try to maintain control over my life. I think many Christians engage in a constant tug-of-war between total control and total surrender. We raise our hands and worship the God who is above it all, but our fists are clenched, hanging on for dear life just in case God drops the ball. Someone once said, "I'm not really a control freak but . . . can I show you the right way to do that?" That someone is often me, foolishly trying to conduct the orchestrator of the entire universe. I live as if I'm saying, "Hey, God, listen . . . I know you're the one who can move heaven and earth, but I was thinking you should move this just a little to the left." God is not sitting up in heaven waiting for me to weigh in on the subject of my life before deciding which direction it should go. From God's eye view, he sees it all, and he's in control of it all. He's got this.

CONTROL VS. CHAOS

One opposite, or antonym, of the word *control* could be the word *chaos*. This is what our minds tell us will break out if our plans don't go the way we want them to go. No one wants chaos. Most of us try to avoid chaos at all cost. But for those who have surrendered their lives and plans to an all-knowing and all-powerful God, giving up control does not mean they are leaving the door open for chaos to break out. Quite the opposite, actually. Chaos is what happens when no one is in control. Calm is what happens when we acknowledge that God is in control. "He calmed the storms with a whisper. The waves of the sea were hushed" (Psalm 107:29 NIV).

When I allow the name "Control Freak" to take ownership of me, I shift my focus from the calmer of storms to the chaos at hand, and I rush to rely on my own ability to control the unexpected situation. I tell myself that if I don't take control, chaos will break out. But as a Christ follower who leaves the reins in God's hands, there can be calm in knowing that God is not a God of chaos but a God of order. "For the LORD is God, and he created the heavens and earth and put everything in place. He made the world to be lived in, not to be a place of empty chaos" (Isaiah 45:18). I think I'm going to make myself a T-shirt that reads, "Dear Control Freak, God is in CONTROL. So don't FREAK!" I'll make one for you too.

Remember how the meteorologist-turned-real-estate-agent said that he now enjoys the changing of the weather? His eyes light up when the clouds roll in. Well, I have another friend, Mike, who shares that same feeling. Mike is a real-life storm chaser. I know you're wondering, *What circle of friends does Matthew run in that he has close ties with a meteorologist and a storm chaser?* You'd think I joined some kind of small group for weather enthusiasts. Sounds like the beginning to a punch line of a bad joke. "Did you hear the one about the singer, the weatherman, and the storm chaser?" Mike lives in an area of the country that sees more than its fair share of foul weather. Twisters, tornados, and hailstorms. He's seen 'em all. And he loves 'em all. While everyone else is running *from* a storm, Mike is one of those guys who hops in his car with his GoPro camera and heads straight toward it. He's even making a reality show chronicling his adventures. Personally, I think he's crazy. But Mike loves it. While others are dreading the storm, he's chasing it down, volunteering for a front-row seat to witness the chaos. Sure, his SUV has a few dents and dings from golf ball–sized hail crashing down on the plains of Texas, but you should see some of the footage his camera captures from the front lines! He describes the whole experience as being an exhilarating adrenaline rush. You never know what will happen. That's the fun part. And while I highly doubt I'll ever share the same enthusiasm for sudden changes in atmospheric pressure, I sure do love the way the calming hands of God lift the pressure from my shoulders in the middle of unexpected changes in my life. When I trust in the only one with God's-eye view, I know that calm will find me, not chaos.

CLOUDY WITH A CHANCE OF CRUSHED DREAMS

"Help! Help! Somebody, please help me!" Falling on the ground in my front yard on the last Friday of July 2002, these were the words I screamed as loudly as I could in the hopes that someone would hear me. Just moments before, I wasn't in need of any help. I had hopped out the door of my eight-hundred-square-foot duplex rental just south of Nashville, ready for a quick afternoon jog. In recent days I had ramped up my exercise routine because in just two short weeks I would be signing my name to my dream-come-true, major-label recording contract. And you know what comes after you sign a record deal? A photo shoot. Hence the afternoon run. This was a season of my life when the only cloud in sight had the number nine assigned to it, and it was *under* my feet. The future was as big, blue, and endless as the sky overhead that particular afternoon, and I was soaking up every minute of a life that was all going according to my plan.

Just as I slammed shut the front door of the duplex, I realized that I had locked myself out. A minor frustration for someone about to sign a *major* record deal. *No problem,* I thought. *I'll just crack open the front window, reach in, and grab my keys from the end table where I set them down.* This was an old house, built in the early 1940s. I quickly detected that the window separating me from my keys and the rest of my day's schedule had most likely remained shut since it was built. Evidently the original owners didn't care for fresh air. This window wasn't sliding up no matter how hard I pushed on the rusty brass sill. Frustrated by the whole sequence of events that had left me stranded on my doorstep, I gave one last shove to try to jar it loose from its rusted resistance. As I did, my left hand slipped from the handle and fell through the thin glass before my reflexes could kick in and stop me. It was too late. Almost immediately I fell into a state of shock as my eyes discovered a deep cut on my left forearm. This next part of the story is one that has made more than one of my friends and family members need to sit down. So I will spare you some of the gory details. Wait, what am I saying? Isn't that what books are for? Details! I found out hours later, after waking up in the emergency room, that the reason I had lost so much blood so fast was because the glass window had severed an artery in my left arm. A little medical lesson here. Might want to write this down: arteries are not supposed to be severed. You'll thank me for that. I found out the hard way.

The details of the days that followed could be aptly set to some seventies psychedelic music while the characters in my story, mostly doctors, moved in and out of my room to the sound of heart-rate monitor beeps and talked in slow-motion nonsense like Charlie Brown's teacher. "Wha-whaa-wha-wha-whaaa . . ." I couldn't tell night from day. Emily, my brand-new girlfriend at the time, sat in a lone chair directly outside of my hospital room through the night and waited for my parents to make the trip from Chicago to be with their son. Family told me later that I would wake in the middle of the night screaming in pain, only to be administered more medication and put back into a deep sleep. I remember the doctors would not allow me to look at my left arm for fear that it would send me into shock again. There were more stitches on my arm than an NFL lineman's jersey. It was a pretty messed-up scene.

As the fog lifted and the immediate shock of this unexpected storm in my life subsided, reality set in like a weight on my chest with every less-than-optimistic word out of the surgeon's mouth. Phrases like "nerve damage," "physical therapy," and "trying to save your hand" fell heavy on the ear of a person planning to use that very hand to sign a recording contract and play guitar for a living. I wasn't chasing this storm. It was chasing me. I can remember the sobering moments in that hospital bed when I was alone with my thoughts, my worries, my fears, and my panic. I remember one such moment vividly when my inner control freak stepped in and made matters worse. I requested a pen and paper from the nurse. Then, with my opposite hand I began to make a list of possible alternate career choices. I really began to panic when I looked at how short the completed list was. It looked something like this:

1. Guy who spins jumbo sign on street corner for mattress store sale.
2. Guy who spins jumbo sign on street corner for jewelry store sale.

That's it. That was where my list started and ended. That's all I had. My dream was slipping through my hands, and at least one of my hands wasn't strong enough to hold on to it even if I could.

HELLO, MY NAME IS "SURRENDER"

My reality changed overnight. So had my prospects. There was no mistaking who *wasn't* in control this time. This control freak had been brought to his knees harder than ever before. My white-knuckle grip had been loosened and instead I was waving a white flag, saying, "Okay, God, I can't fix this. I need you. You win." But you see, that's one of the amazing things I learned about God during this painful change of plans. God wasn't allowing this just so I would be brutally brought to my knees and admit defeat. This was never about God putting me in my place. God knows that the closest you and I will ever get to seeing from a God's-eye view is when we are on our knees. I surrendered in the hospital bed. I surrendered all of my fears and questions and anger and control. And guess what I began to feel long before my hand started to heal? Calmness.

From little interruptions in our daily plans to foundation-shaking and heartbreaking trials that blindside us, I'm willing to bet you've experienced both. We all will at some point in our lives. God's plan for you is that any sudden turn of events will lead to a sudden turn of your heart in the direction to the one who is never surprised by anything that ever happens. Through my own painful trial, I gained a greater glimpse of what God was up to. I learned that God can use our unwanted change of plans to give us four things: a wake-up call, a break-up call, a shake-up call, and a take-up call. Here's what I mean.

A Wake-up Call is that moment when we realize that our best efforts, schemes, and plans can't fix the situations we're in. We can be the biggest control freaks ever, but we're never in control. We don't want these reminders, which is precisely why we need these reminders. The unexpected trials and changes in our circumstances leave us helpless and remind us what Jesus meant when he said, "Apart from me you can do nothing" (John 15:5).

A Break-up Call for me was when I was stuck in that hospital bed with a depressingly short list of other possible career choices. I had to break up with all of the plans I had been making for my music and my career, and I had to come to grips with the possibility that my hands might never be able to grip a guitar as they used to. Would I be okay if this thing I loved so much was taken away from me? Did I trust that God knew what he was doing? "In their hearts humans plan their course, but the LORD establishes their steps" (Proverbs 16:9 NIV).

A Shake-up Call is the unexpected and unwanted toppling of our daily or even life goals, but we do not have to be shaken when this happens. The one who allows the storms to rage is the same one who calms the storm. "He alone is my rock and my salvation, my fortress where I will not be shaken" (Psalm 62:6).

A Take-up Call challenges us to see every change as an invitation to take up a new perspective on our plans and the one who is in control at all times. When we do, we might actually wind up understanding what my friend the meteorologist said about enjoying the changing weather as he did in his childhood. Taking up the belief that God works miraculously in unexpected ways will wake us up each day with a sense of excitement and anticipation to see what unplanned moments he has planned for us. Seeing the way God works allows for a monumental shift in the mentality of any control freak. "No ear has heard and no eye has seen a God like you, who works for those who wait for him" (Isaiah 64:4).

I did eventually sign that record deal. With my right hand. And that girl I was dating, who slept outside of my hospital room? Well, you don't let a girl who's seen you at your worst (in a hospital gown) get away. We were married a year later. After a year of painful recovery, I regained most of the feeling in my fingers. I never did enter into the world of sign spinning for mattress stores. Instead, you'll find me on stage with a guitar in my hands. But these days, there's a seven-inch scar that runs down the length of my forearm. It's a permanent reminder of the day a control freak was brought to his knees and found out that's not such a bad place to be. Every time I look down at my guitar or raise my hands in worship, that scar reminds me not to live my life with clenched fists but with outstretch arms, giving up control to the one who's really in control.

You, too, can loosen your grip now, no matter what situation you find yourself in. God's got this, and you can trust him. "I know what I'm doing. I have it all planned out—plans to take care of you, not abandon you, plans to give you the future you hope for" (Jeremiah 29:11 MSG).

On a scale of 1 to 10, how much of a control freak are you? What does your need for control say about your trust in God?

How has God used unwanted changes of plans to give you a wake-up call, a break-up call, a shake-up call, and a take-up call?

Read Jeremiah 29:11. You've probably read that verse a hundred times, but how much do you believe in God's promise there—especially when the future looks bleak from our point of view?

CHAPTER 4

MAY I PLEASE HAVE THE LANGUAGE OF ORIGIN?

If you aren't in over your head,
how do you know how tall you are?

T. S. ELIOT

An elementary school gymnasium that smelled of Lunchables, applesauce, and awkwardness. A whispering crowd of students seated by grade in rows on the floor placing bets on who would be eliminated first. A fidgeting group of finalists in metal folding chairs at one end of the gym waiting for their names to be called. This was the scene of the fated sixth-grade spelling bee that will forever live on in infamy. There I was, seated among the finalists that afternoon. Sweaty palms. Shaky knees. Bloodshot eyes from staying up late the night before (and several nights before that) tearing through the pages of the dictionary as if my life depended on it. I knew how to spell *catawampus* and *cauliflower* and *hyperbole* and *hypnosis*. I knew to always put *i* before *e* except after *c*, and that *u* always comes after *q*. Yeah, I was coming in pretty confident. But that quickly changed as the moments inched closer to the beginning of the battle.

I am so ready for this!

I think I'm ready for this.

Am I ready for this?

Oh man, I'm not ready for this!

Wait, how do I spell cat?

Oh no! I'm going to get crushed.

I have to pee!

Dear God, if you help me out this one time, I promise I'll never ask for anything else . . .

In a matter of minutes, I had gone from totally ready to utterly unraveled. My confidence had curdled like one of those small 2% milk cartons you forgot in your lunch box for a couple of days. By the looks of it, I wasn't the only one beginning to cave under the pressure. There were quite a few other students on that stage turning whiter shades of pale and looking as if they needed a pass to visit the nurse. But there was no turning back now. The judges shushed the student body, read the rules to us, and the spelling bee began. The next section of this story could be titled "Dropping Like Flies." Because that's what happened. It was brutal. One misspelled word after another.

Kids stalled the best they could, but it was easy to tell when one didn't know the word thrown at them. "Umm . . . Can I have the definition of the word?" "Hmm . . . Uh, yeah . . . can you please use it in a sentence?" These questions were only delaying the judges' inevitable response. "I'm sorry, but that is incorrect. You've been disqualified." I watched as one contestant after another—with shoulders slumped and dreams dashed—slowly made the walk of shame from that microphone to their lowly place on the sticky gym floor with the rest of their classmates.

And then there were two. Don't ask me how it happened, but I was one of them. Making it to the final round was more than even *I* had hoped for. I can't remember what words I spelled correctly to get that far into the competition. I like to think the reason for this is because I was in what the sports world calls "the zone." Just as what occurs for an elite athlete, I was hyperfocused, the game slowed down in my mind, and my skills shifted into that elusive extra gear. I was exhibiting that special something that just couldn't be explained. That intangible greatness that propels one to higher heights than any other player on the field, or on the court, or . . . on the spelling bee stage. Like Michael Jordan in game one of the 1992 NBA Finals. He was unstoppable in the first half. No one could guard him. In fact, he set records for an NBA Finals half: thirty-five points, and six three-point shots. After he hit his sixth shot from "down town," cameras caught him shrugging his shoulders with a look of disbelief on his sweaty face. Even he was surprised by his greatness. That's "the zone" I believe I was in the day of that spelling bee.

My spelling skills were hitting nothing but net, word after word after word. I have to say, the moment I felt certain I would emerge the champion of the spelling bee was when I noticed the only other contestant left on stage. *She* was a fourth grader! Are you kidding me? Fourth. Grade. Girl. Instantly, my chest puffed out and I transformed into some kind of sixth-grade Goliath. In my mind, I was laughing and mocking the entire fourth-grade class. "AM I A DOG THAT YOU WOULD COME AT ME WITH A STICK?" In no time at all, I had gone from underdog to crowd favorite. If this spelling bee had taken place in Vegas, no gambler would dare bet against me. But something happened. Perhaps I had overlooked my opponent. (This was easy to do because she was shorter than me.) When I lowered my sights and caught the look in her eye, I could tell this was no ordinary fourth grader. There was a fire in her eyes. A determination. A look on her face that said, "Go ahead, underestimate me. But this girl is about to run over you, and I'll be the one hoisting that golden trophy overhead while this crowd applauds. You, sir, are going down!" Sure, to the rest of the room she might have seemed like a sweet, smiley, pigtail-wearing fourth grader. Maybe I was the only one close enough to see it, but that look in her eyes sent shivers down my spine. This girl meant business. She was spelling words and taking names.

Final round: She was up first. She nailed it. Spelled her word with ease and grace. The crowd applauded. She smiled in a show of innocent appreciation and then turned back to her seat. As she passed me I was pretty sure I heard her whisper, "Let's see if you can beat that, loser." There was a real Jekyll and Hyde thing going on with her. If I had been in "the zone" earlier in the contest, I now felt as though I were in the middle of the Bermuda

Triangle, headed toward a most certain demise. I wasn't sure I could spell my own name if asked to. Man, fourth graders can really get in your head. "Matthew, it's your turn." I heard my name called and felt nothing but fear. "Your word is *impossible*."

Oh, the irony, I thought. And in sixth grade I didn't even know what the word *irony* meant. That's how ironic this sequence of events was shaping up to be. Deep breath. Then a few more deep breaths. "I-M-P-O-S-S . . . um, can I please have the language of origin?" (As if that was going to help me spell this mammoth of a four-syllable word.) I knew it wasn't going to help. I was simply stalling as I had seen so many fallen spellers before me do on the way to their inevitable defeat. I was frantically combing through every corner of my brain to see if somehow, somewhere I had remembered how to spell the word. Time was running out. My fellow classmates in the audience began to whisper. I could feel my face turning a bright shade of embarrassment. And that fourth-grade girl was sitting right behind me all the while, just ready and waiting to pounce and devour her weak competition the moment I slipped up.

"I-M-P-O-S-S-I . . ." *Keep it together, West. You're almost there.* " . . . B-O-L. IMPOSSIBOL."

"I'm sorry, but that is incorrect." The words from the judge hit hard, hammering the final nail in the coffin that sealed the death of my hopes and dreams of going down in history as the greatest speller ever to walk the halls of Willow Creek Elementary School. The word *impossible* proved to be, well, impossible for me to overcome that day. For the rest of that school year, I was doomed to be known as the sixth-grade boy who was out-spelled by a fourth-grade girl. So much for being in "the zone."

HELLO, MY NAME IS "AFRAID"

What I wouldn't give for the chance to travel back to a time when a spelling bee was the most "impossible" circumstance I might face in a day. The stakes get much higher as we get older, don't they? What's the impossible staring you right in the eye today? Perhaps you've been dealing with an impossible for some time now. You're awakened in the middle of the night by a call from the police station asking to speak to you because your prodigal son is in trouble. FEAR. Sitting in the waiting room at your doctor's office, you hear the nurse call your name as she holds the results of your CT scan. FEAR. Creditors are calling around the clock with threats of financial ruin if you don't pay what you owe, but there is no job in sight. FEAR. FEAR. FEAR. Impossible circumstances are often the reason why the name "Afraid" occupies so many nametags. But simply knowing you're not alone offers little consolation and encouragement.

Joshua was afraid. Yeah, I know what you're thinking. Isn't that the guy who marched around Jericho for seven days and then made the walls come crumbling down by blowing on some horns? Yep, that's the one. You'd think we would be dealing with a pretty confident dude. I mean, who agrees to bring horns instead of weapons to a battle? Certainly, this could not be the work of some scaredy-cat. But before he ever fought and won the battle of Jericho, Joshua was just a wide-eyed, newly appointed leader of the Israelites. After Moses had died, God picked Joshua to be the one to lead his people to the promised land. How do we know he was scared? In Joshua 1:9, God told Joshua to "be strong and courageous! Do not be afraid or discouraged" (NIV). This wasn't some blanket statement in case Joshua was scared at any point. God knows his children's thoughts and speaks directly to them. He knew what Joshua was thinking and feeling in those very moments, and he spoke the words he knew a scared Joshua must have needed to hear before facing his impossible. There have been times I have said the same to my children. "Don't be afraid." Why would I feel the need to speak those three words of comfort? Chances are, I could see fear in their eyes or sense trepidation. A parent picks up on these things. God picked up on Joshua's fear and spoke right to it.

Now, it's one thing to tell someone, "Don't be afraid." But that is one instruction that must be followed with a why. If someone tells me, "Don't pick up that poisonous snake," I don't need a reason why. And I don't need to be told twice. I know if I pick up that snake, I'll soon be falling down like those Jericho walls—hard and fast. But if I am struck with fear in the middle of an impossible situation, it's not going to be enough for someone to simply say, "Don't be afraid." You better give me a reason why. Better yet, you better *show* me a reason why!

When one of my daughters was learning how to swim, I would stand in the pool and say to her, "Don't be afraid," but I wouldn't stop there, because if I had, she'd have had a hand on her hip and a distrusting look that said, *Sure, easy for you to say.* So to reassure her, I would say something like, "I'm right here, and I'm going to catch you." Then I would hold out my arms to show her what I meant. The fear would be replaced by faith in me, and she would jump in. This is what God offered Joshua—a why. "Do not be afraid or discouraged. *For the LORD your God is with you wherever you go*" (Joshua 1:9, emphasis mine). God gave Joshua a reason *not* to be afraid: he was going to be with Joshua wherever he led him. But God didn't stop there. He went on to *show* Joshua, to prove his faithfulness, by miraculously making a way through the Jordan River and then by fulfilling the promise that Jericho's walls would fall.

You'd think after witnessing those victories firsthand, "Afraid" would have been long gone from Joshua's nametag. But guess what happened just a few short chapters later? The Israelites lost a battle. Joshua was once again scared and crying out for help. God issued a similar refrain to Joshua's fear-filled heart: "Do not be afraid or discouraged" (8:1). Sound familiar? It didn't matter how many trials he had already overcome. When faced with a new impossible, fear still overcame Joshua. Am I the only one who is strangely comforted by the thought that even Joshua had recurring bouts with fear? We are humans. Humans in need of reminders. David wrote, "When I am afraid, I will put my trust in you" (Psalm 56:3). Notice the grace extended to us in this scripture. "*When* I am afraid." Not, "*If* I am afraid." We *will* have times when the impossible mountains in our way threaten to once again turn our faith into fear. But just as he did with Joshua, God will meet us there in the middle of that fear, saying, "Do not be afraid or discouraged. For the LORD your God is with you wherever you go."

So, how can we take off that nametag that says "Afraid" and keep it off? Well, even though Joshua had his moments, his instincts were right. When his army was brutally defeated, he did two things we can learn from and repeat. He *prayed* and then he *obeyed*. First, he called out to God in prayer, tearing his clothes in dismay while crying out, "Oh, Sovereign LORD . . ." (7:7). The word *sovereign* means "supreme leader," and the word *Lord* means someone or something having power, authority, or influence. Sure, Joshua was afraid. His army had just been brutally defeated. But he knew that the God he was calling on had the ultimate power to see him through his latest impossible fight.

NO WAY, NINEVEH

When you are afraid, do you believe that you have a sovereign Lord who is looking out for you, ready to help you? If deep down you don't believe this, then you will likely find yourself filled with fear and running away from challenges, not toward them. Like Jonah did. God called him to minister to the people in Nineveh, a city that was an absolute mess. This was a pretty scary scene. God described the people there by saying, "They're in a bad way and I can't ignore it any longer" (Jonah 1:2 MSG). But instead of obeying God, Scripture says in the next verse that "Jonah got up and went the other direction."

Obedience *to* God is the truest evidence of trust *in* God. Jonah heard God. But Jonah didn't trust God, so he disobeyed.

If Jonah had truly trusted that God knew what he was doing when he told him to travel to minister to the crazies in Nineveh, wouldn't he have obeyed God's instructions knowing that he was in control? Jonah was more than just a little afraid. I think it's interesting that the Bible tells us just how far off course Jonah chose to travel in response to God's call—the other direction. It's not like he thought to himself, *Well, maybe I'll go to the town* next *to Nineveh and commute back and forth*, or *Perhaps God meant another town that starts with* N. No, he wasn't even attempting to come close to obeying God's directions. Jonah tried to get "as far away from GOD as he could get" (v. 3 MSG). If God had said to go north, Jonah had headed south. That's what fear will do to you. It'll send you scrambling, running for the hills. Or in Jonah's case, running for the whales.

Fear itself is not a bad thing. It's a human thing. Nelson Mandela said, "The brave man is not he who does not feel afraid, but he who conquers that fear." How we handle the fear we face in our lives is what's important. Joshua faced fear, and so did Jonah. Fear is the litmus test for trust. Joshua passed that test. When his army lost the battle and he was afraid they would be conquered, *he prayed.* Jonah failed his test. When God called him to go to a place that scared him, *he strayed.* Both were faced with the impossible, both felt fear, and both found out their level of trust in God.

If Jonah had trusted God more than his own view of the circumstances, he would have obeyed God, traveled to reach the people in Nineveh, and saved himself a lot of trouble. We know what happened as a result of Jonah's running. Soon he was swimming in the belly of whale and sinking in an ocean of more fear. Now, I don't know this for certain, but I think Jonah's prayer while in the belly of that whale might actually be the first ever anxiety attack in history. Can you imagine? I've been on a whale-watching excursion in Alaska, and even being within a couple hundred feet of one of God's largest creations sent a chill down my spine. If I were Jonah, I would have been freaking out too. Well, the Bible records Jonah's "freak out," which comes in the form of a prayer. Ironic, isn't it? Fear sent him running from God in the first place, but fortunately a greater fear sent him running back to God in Jonah 2:5–6 (MSG):

> Ocean gripped me by the throat. The ancient abyss grabbed me and held tight. My head was all tangled in seaweed at the bottom of the sea . . . I was as far down as a body can go, and the gates were slamming shut behind me forever.

Just reading Jonah's deep-sea description makes me feel a little anxious too. Anxiety is a descendant of fear. The two are related. They're part of the same dysfunctional family of stress-filled emotions that can occupy our nametags and control our lives. An anxiety attack is a feeling of immense, impending doom. It's a feeling like everything around us is breaking down or that we are about to die.

According to the National Institute of Mental Health, anxiety has become the number one mental health issue in North America. It's estimated that one-third of the population experiences anxiety issues. I see the evidence of this statistic in my travels around the country and in the countless stories people share with me. Where does their fear and anxiety come from? Well, one thing I know is that fear and anxiety are not from God, for the Bible says that "God has not given us a spirit of fear and timidity, but of power, love, and self-discipline" (2 Timothy 1:7). No, fear is on the list of Satan's favorite things. Doesn't matter what kind of evil he's cooking up to drag you down, fear is one of those go-to ingredients he rarely leaves out. A reason for this is because fear is a gateway to so many other false identities that weigh us down. Anxiety is one of them. When faced with your impossible, Satan loves to send you on a downward spiral:

Faith into fear
Fear into anxiety
Anxiety into discouragement
Discouragement into depression
Depression into hopelessness

Perhaps you are all too familiar with that paralyzing progression of emotions. As seen in the lives of Joshua and Jonah, God offers us a way to reverse it: pray and obey. When they did both of those things, God faithfully saved them. God also knows Satan's plan to get your fear to spill over into anxiety and has offered you a way to fight back.

God wants you to take your eyes off of whatever is making you afraid and anxious right now and look to him. Just as God offered Joshua a why when telling him not to be afraid, he offers you a reason why you don't have to be anxious. Scripture says, "Do not be anxious about anything, but in everything by prayer and supplication with thanksgiving let your requests be made known to God. And the peace of God, which surpasses all understanding, will guard your hearts and minds in Christ Jesus" (Philippians 4:6–7 ESV). In the middle of your most fear-filled moment, when you reach out to God, he will give you *peace*. And this gift of peace is not just some fluffy, feel-good moment of forgetfulness. This peace is an armed guard. This peace protects you from the fear and anxiety Satan uses to attack. This peace is powerful enough to reverse Satan's spiral of fear.

A HUG AND A WHISPER

At most of my concerts, I invite people to join me for a pre-show question-and-answer session. This time is made available for a select group of concertgoers. I believe the term for this group of people is *VIP*. For some reason these very important people actually think it would be fun to hang out with me. They even pay money for this. I know, crazy. (Unless you're one of those people and you're reading this right now. In that case, I think you are really smart and intelligent, and I thank you for your support.) I just have a hard time believing that people would pay to hang out with me, because it is a much different picture in my family. In my own home, I pretty much have to pay my children to hang out with *me*. But somehow this does not make me a VIP in their eyes.

At any rate, this event before the concert usually winds up

being a special time when I get to interact with some of my most faithful supporters, share a bit more of my story, and even hear some of their stories. During a recent preshow event, a young eleven-year-old child raised his hand to ask a question. The emcee made his way over to the boy and handed him the microphone.

"Hey, buddy, what's your question for me?"

"Can I have a hug?" he asked.

A bit surprised by this request but more than happy to oblige, I said, "Well, sure!" and then stood at the foot of the stage with my arms opened wide as that little boy made his way down the aisle. He ran up to me, gave me a big hug. But then he didn't let go. He had his arms around my waist and was squeezing me so tightly. So I bent down to hug the little boy in return, and as I did he whispered something in my ear that made tears well up in my eyes and forget there was a crowd in front of us.

"Um, I have a lot of anxiety," he softly said, "and your song 'Strong Enough' really helps me. When I hear you sing, 'Hands of mercy, won't you cover me,' I feel God's hands holding me, and I feel better."

At that, he released his grip on me and walked back to his seat in the second row. Just a kid. A child. A little boy who should be smiling, laughing, and rough-housing with his friends. A kid who shouldn't have a care in the world. Instead, for reasons I never found out, he's a young boy with the whole world on his shoulders. Whatever he is going through, it's enough to teach a kid what the word *anxiety* even means, and it breaks my heart even as I write this story now.

That night after the show was over, I prayed for the boy before falling asleep. As the tour bus headed to the next city, my thoughts were still back with him. I wondered what kind of home life he was returning to after the concert. I wondered what might have been going on in his family or at school to make him feel such fear and anxiety. I prayed that the "hands of mercy" he spoke of would indeed squeeze him tightly and tenderly as he, too, laid his head on his pillow that night. I asked God to replace the anxiety and worries in his little world with the innocence and joy and happiness that every child should get to experience before the real world turns them into grown-ups.

I think about that little boy often. That hug and that whisper in my ear. And when I do, it makes me think about how our heavenly Father greets *us* with a hug and a whisper too. When the word *impossible* grips our hearts with fear, he wraps his hands of mercy around us and whispers, "Do not be afraid . . . For the LORD your God is with you wherever you go."

Obedience *to* God is the truest evidence of trust *in* God, so . . . are you running away from challenges or toward them?

When have you felt yourself on a downward spiral, progressing from faith . . . to fear . . . to anxiety . . . to discouragement . . . to depression . . . to hopelessness?

Read Joshua 1:9. What's it going to take to turn this verse from being words that go in one ear and out the other to a promise that penetrates your heart and gives you confidence and peace?

CHAPTER 5

LOVE, THE EASTER BUNNY

My son told me that the Tooth Fairy, Easter Bunny, and Santa Claus do not exist, and he really upset me, because I understood that my life is a lie.

UNKNOWN

Being a parent is hard work. And sometimes I just make it harder on myself. I feel this pressure to nurture and protect my children's sense of wonder and imagination for as long as possible. But this can be exhausting. We've got the Tooth Fairy, who leaves money under the pillow; the Easter Bunny, who never fails to deliver a basket of chocolates; the leprechauns, who always leave Kelly-green pee in the toilet on St. Patrick's Day; and of course Santa with his reindeer, who better show up by Christmas morning, filling those stockings and finishing off the plate of cookies. Now, at Christmastime we even have this elf that sits on a shelf, watching their every move and reporting back to Santa how the kids are behaving (pretty creepy, now that I think of it). Honestly, I have a hard time keeping track of all of these fairy tales with my children . . . and recently that caught up with me.

My daughter had been on a hot streak with one wiggly tooth after another falling out. Well, the "Tooth Fairy" was working overtime and forgot to visit one night. Lulu woke up the next morning with her little tooth still under her pillow and no dollar bill lying there as she had hoped there would be. I remember being woken up by my frantic wife as she ran into our bedroom, shook me, and said, "YOU FORGOT?! HOW COULD YOU FORGET TO LEAVE HER MONEY UNDER THE PILLOW?!" As the fog lifted from my mind, reality sank in that this could be the end of my daughter's childlike wonder if I didn't think fast. So that's what I did.

I quickly scribbled a note using my opposite hand, explaining to Lulu that I, the Tooth Fairy, thought it would be fun to hide her dollar somewhere in her house so she could have a fun time searching for it. My wife hid a dollar discretely behind a couch cushion, and then I emerged from my bedroom with this newly discovered letter that was addressed to Lulu. She was so excited to see this letter and began to read it aloud in the kitchen as I turned my back to prepare breakfast. As she read my . . . er, I mean, the Tooth Fairy's note, I began patting myself on the back, thinking, *Nice job, Dad. You really saved the day.* Just about the time I was sure disaster had been successfully averted, Lulu read the end of the letter: "Love, the Easter Bunny."

My gloating came to a screeching halt. She read it again, only this time in the form of a puzzled question: "Love, the

Easter Bunny?" She looked at me and asked, "Daddy, why would the Easter Bunny be visiting me and not the Tooth Fairy?" I stopped scrambling the eggs I had been cooking and began scrambling to think of an explanation. Thankfully, before I could even find the shovel to dig myself out of this hole, Lulu came up with her own solution. "You know, I bet the Tooth Fairy has been so busy because lots of my friends have lost a tooth too. Isn't that so cool that the Easter Bunny helped him out?" "Yes, honey," I said with a sigh, "that Easter Bunny is a real class act."

GOD IS NOT A FAIRY TALE

I know. I am setting up my kids for quite the letdown when they realize the Easter Bunny and all of their other seasonal heroes are fictional fairy tales. I remember holding a momentary youthful grudge toward my parents when it finally dawned on me that "Santa Claus" bared too much of a resemblance to my dad to be mere coincidence. I'm pretty sure I hid the tears in my eyes as I shouted something resembling the words of Buddy the Elf, who refused to settle for a shopping mall Santa: "You sit on a throne of lies!"

As a kid, I'm not sure I saw much of a difference between God, the Easter Bunny, or Santa. To my adolescent mind, they did have more than a few things in common:

1. I couldn't see them.
2. If I was good, they would bring me things.
3. I heard a lot more about them around the holidays.

In time, the fairy tales of childhood inevitably reveal themselves for what they are: fairy tales. And in our lives, God reveals himself for who he is. Unlike the crushing disappointment that comes from finding out our parents ate all of Santa's cookies, the opposite occurs when the curtain is pulled back and the eyes of our hearts are opened to this revealing truth: God is not a fairy tale. There is no letdown when he shows himself for who he really is. Instead, there comes the overwhelming sense that though he might not be seen with the physical eye, he is real.

A. W. Pink wrote, "Happy the soul that has been awed by a view of God's majesty." Can you think of a moment when God revealed himself to you and you became certain he was real? That moment is different for everyone. I'm talking about the moment or moments when his presence, his power, or his love were simply undeniable and the evidence in front of you forced the dams built by doubt to give way to a flood of faith. The head and the heart are at once aligned and agreeing in unison, "I may not see him, but I know he's real."

It's the ultrasound a young couple gazes at excitedly as the doctor says, "Looks like you're going to have a girl" . . . *God is not a fairy tale.*

It's the breathtaking sunrise from thirty thousand feet through an airplane window on an early-morning business trip that causes a man to state, "There's no way this could have been created by mere human hands" . . . *God is not a fairy tale.*

It's the unexplainable peace that washes over a woman even after she receives a heartbreaking diagnosis that should have rocked her world . . . *God is not a fairy tale.*

It's the pounding in your heart you felt when you heard the preacher ask, "Is there anyone who wants to say yes to Jesus tonight?" . . . *God is not a fairy tale.*

I received a story from a man named Lajos, who described the life-changing moment God became real to him:

> I grew up in Communist Hungary and escaped in 1987 at age twenty-one. I used to be an atheist who mocked Christians. I spent eighteen months of my life in a refugee camp. I went into the camp as an atheist unbeliever and eighteen months later I came out of it turning my life over to Christ. It was a trying, dramatic, and sometimes traumatic experience. But in the middle of what should have been my most hopeless days and nights, I could not deny the overwhelming feeling that I was not alone, and the peace that came along with it.

God is not a fairy tale. And just as he revealed himself to Lajos, an atheist who once considered Christians fools for believing in a fictional savior, God has been making himself known since the beginning of creation. "For ever since the world was created, people have seen the earth and sky. Through everything God made, they can clearly see his invisible qualities—his eternal power and divine nature. So they have no excuse for not knowing God" (Romans 1:20).

The more I think about it, the Bible is really one story after another of God becoming real and making himself known to his people. He became real to Saul, who was on his way to

Damascus to "kill the Lord's followers" (Acts 9:1), when a light from heaven knocked him to the ground. God was saying, "I have other plans for you." He became real to the Israelites by miraculously parting the Jordan River for them to cross until "the whole nation was across the Jordan, and not one wet foot" (Joshua 3:17 MSG). He became real to a leper with one healing touch (Matthew 8) and real to Moses with one burning bush (Exodus 3). God became real to a doubting Thomas when he appeared to his disciple, saying, "Put your finger here; see my hands. Reach out your hand and put it into my side. Stop doubting and believe" (John 20:27 NIV). God became real to all of humanity by sending his only Son, Jesus, to walk among us. "So the Word became human and made his home among us. He was full of unfailing love and faithfulness. And we have seen his glory, the glory of the Father's one and only son" (John 1:14). And God is on a mission to become real to you. Why? Because your search to find the real *you* starts with finding him.

I love how *The Message* paraphrases Colossians 2:9–10: "Everything of God gets expressed in him, so you can see and hear him clearly. You don't need a telescope, a microscope, or a horoscope to realize the fullness of Christ, and the emptiness of the universe without him. When you come to him, that fullness comes together for you, too. His power extends over everything." God's desire is for you and me to see and hear him clearly. With this scripture he is saying, "The search to find the real you in this world will come up empty until I become real *to* you." Unlike a Santa Claus for hire hoping you won't tug on his beard to find out it's factory-made, God has nothing to hide and wants nothing more than for you to see the real him, know the real him, and believe in the real him. I thought I knew God. But it wasn't until I went through one of the toughest times of my life that he became more real to me than ever before.

A SEASON OF SILENCE

I always liked the story of Zachariah the priest, but I never dreamed I'd wind up having so much in common with him. Zachariah and his wife, Elizabeth, had lived long lives that were pleasing to God, but they were never able to have children. An angel appeared to Zachariah, saying, "Don't fear, Zachariah. Your prayer has been heard. Elizabeth, your wife, will bear a son by you. You are to name him John. You're going to leap like a gazelle for joy, and not only you—many will delight in his birth. He'll achieve great stature with God" (Luke 1:13–14 MSG). Zachariah was a man who believed in God, but he found this angel's message to be, simply, unbelievable. He responded to the angel's news by saying, "Do you expect me to believe this? I'm an old man and my wife is an old woman" (v. 18). Zachariah heard the angel say "leap like a gazelle," and thought to himself, *I'm so old, I'm more likely to sleep than leap.* But the angel said, "I am Gabriel, the sentinel of God, sent especially to bring you this glad news. But because you won't believe me, you'll be unable to say a word until the day of your son's birth. Every word I've spoken to you will come true on time—God's time" (vv. 19–20). God revealed himself to Zachariah through the angel and he missed it. Now he would have to spend the next several months in silence, missing his voice. That's where the similarities between Zachariah and me begin.

In 2007 I, too, spent months in complete silence. My wife jokes that it was the greatest two months of our marriage. Imagine trying to win an argument with your spouse while armed with nothing but a dry-erase board. The only way I could get my point across was to try and write with all capital letters. "I DO NOT WANT CHICKEN FOR DINNER!" But who was I kidding? We were going to have chicken no matter how big those letters were.

The reason for my silence? Three words that are often the kiss of death for a singer: *vocal cord surgery*. Many careers have fallen under the knife only to fall off of the music industry's radar shortly after. A hemorrhaged blood vessel had caused my left vocal cord to become completely paralyzed, and after weeks of rest the doctors informed me that surgery was my only option. My concerts were canceled indefinitely. My songwriting appointments too. I couldn't make any progress in the recording studio on my next record. Kind of need a voice to do that. Everything came to a screeching halt as I was forced to wait. Wait in silence.

I don't like silence. On my list of least favorite things, being alone with my thoughts would be right near the top. Up until the day I lost my voice, I avoided silence at all costs. When driving my car, I'd keep the radio on. Going for a walk? Might as well put my headphones in and listen to a podcast. If alone in my house, I'd keep the television on just to keep me company. I think most people prefer noise, commotion, and conversation over silence, solitude, and isolation any day of the week. Even prisons use solitary confinement as one of their harshest penalties, attempting to keep inmates in line. Silence is scary. Solitude is uncomfortable. Isolation makes me restless. Even the thought of being alone with my thoughts is something I don't like to think about!

Henri Nouwen wrote, "As soon as we are alone . . . inner chaos opens up in us. This chaos can be so disturbing and so confusing that we can hardly wait to get busy again." Yet, with my voice taken away and me becoming some kind of modern-day Zachariah, I had no choice but to succumb to silence and enter into the chaos of my mind and heart that I typically had tried so hard to avoid. It was there, right smack-dab in the middle of my silent chaos, where God became real to me as never before. And it all started with eight words in a Bible verse I had read a thousand times before: "Be still, and know that I am God!" (Psalm 46:10).

Be Still

I had learned this scripture as a child, but I found myself reading it with new eyes and understooding it with new clarity during my personal season of silence. Another translation begins, "Cease striving" (NASB). This is a call to enter into that uncomfortable "chaos" of silence. Being unable to speak, I found myself not wanting to be around people. One-way conversations are not much fun. Instead, I retreated to my music room far away from the rest of our home and spent hours a day by myself, writing in my journal and pouring out my heart and worries and fears and anxieties and questions on the page. That music room may never have been quieter, but the chaos in my mind was at times deafening.

Turns out, every time I snuck away to my silent retreat, I was entering into a different kind of one-way conversation— one that we all desperately need to be a part of: a one-way conversation with God. This time my voice was silenced. But his voice came in louder and clearer than I had ever experienced before in the form of those two words. When the inner chaos of my forced silence felt too much to bear, he would return to me over and over like a calming whisper keeping the chaos at bay, "Be still." The more I dared to resist my restless tendencies and obey that instruction, the more I sensed there was a reason for my silence, something I was about to discover. Something that was going to change my life. Something that would make this struggle with solitude worthwhile. Ironic, isn't it? Once I stopped talking, I heard God.

And Know

To *know* means to be aware of something through observation. The psalmist's encouragement to be still had a purpose behind it. Be still so that you can observe and learn. In other words, "Watch and learn." Mother Teresa wrote,

> In the silence of the heart God speaks. If you face God in prayer and silence, God will speak to you. Then you will know that you are nothing. It is only when you realize your nothingness, your emptiness, that God can

fill you with himself. Souls of prayer are souls of great silence.

In my silence, I realized that God was getting my attention. Like Zachariah, who's doubt and disbelief had gotten in the way of an encounter with God, my own voice had been getting in the way and fooling me into thinking I was something special. Losing the very thing that you thought made you special is a leveling experience. I was known for my music. My name was only recognizable, respected, or highly regarded because of the voice and the songs I sang with that voice. Without it, I felt like nothing. And like Mother Teresa described, my awareness of my nothingness blew the door wide open for God to step in and reveal himself to me in a powerful way.

See, God loves us too much to let us get in the way of what he wants to show us. And what he wants to show us is *him*! Whenever God feels distant, he is never the reason for that distance. Whether or not we experience a real encounter with a real God rests squarely on our shoulders. Success, possessions, relationships, intellect, priorities, choices, or even our own voice is what gets in the way. Out of his deep love for us, God is willing to allow even those things which we hold on to dearly to fall away in order to make room for this revelation: our real-world problems need a real-world God. Since calling out to Adam and Eve in the garden of Eden, he has been cutting through the cluttered and noisy lives of his children in a million different ways, but always with the same message: "Be still, and know . . ."

That I Am God

Zachariah thought there was no way he and his wife could have a child in their old age. In his season of silence, he discovered that God is who he says he is and does what he says he will do. His wife did give birth to a son, just as the angel had promised. Everything happened exactly as God had planned, and Zachariah stood by, a silent witness to a real God performing a real miracle in his life. Scripture says that the moment his doubt faded, his voice returned. What was the first thing he did with his newly restored vocal cords? "Instantly Zechariah could speak again, and *he began praising God*" (Luke 1:64, emphasis mine).

I, too, have been a silent witness to a God who is anything but a fairy tale. During my trial, I began to ask God for help. After all, I was faced with the reality that I had nothing and that I could do nothing to fix my circumstance. As I continued to "be still," my prayer evolved from one of asking God to fix my situation to asking him to reveal himself to me.

In MY real fear, I found HIS real presence . . . "The LORD your God is in your midst, a mighty one who will save; he will rejoice over you with gladness; he will quiet you by his love; he will exult over you with loud singing." (Zephaniah 3:17 ESV)

In MY real weakness, I found HIS real power . . . "Fear not, for I am with you; do not be dismayed, for I am your God; I will strengthen you, I will help you, I will uphold you with my righteous right hand." (Isaiah 41:10 ESV)

And in MY real confusion, I found HIS real plan... "But the LORD's plans stand firm forever; his intentions can never be shaken." (Psalm 33:11)

As God answered my prayers, he made things very clear about who he is: Real presence. Real power. Real Purpose. Real God.

HELLO, MY NAME IS "BELIEVER"

I remember stepping back into the vocal booth of the recording studio for the first time in nearly a year to pick up my paralyzed dream again. Through the entire trial and season of silence, the voice and the presence of God had become so real to me. I had already believed in God before those dark and silent days in the music room. But any doubt that had been hiding in the corners of my heart had been pushed out by the power of God's presence that met me when I learned to be still.

Now that the wheels of life had begun to slowly turn in forward motion, I was almost sad to be stepping out of my season of silence, because I didn't want to lose what I had experienced from that prolonged encounter with my own nothingness and God's everythingness—the heightened awareness and recognition of the sound of his voice and the promise of his hand on my life. The first song I sang when my voice returned echoed the same response of praise Zachariah gave the day God restored his voice:

You're everything good in my life
Everything honest and true
And all of those stars hanging up in the sky
Could never shine brighter than You

God promises in Jeremiah 29:13–14, "You will seek me and find me when you seek me with all your heart. I will be found by you" (NIV). God is not a fairy tale. God is not hiding. He is real, he is alive, and he is on a mission to make a believer out of you. Perhaps you've never encountered God in a real way. Perhaps you find yourself wondering if he's real. Perhaps you believe in God, but you've never dared to seek him with "all your heart." I invite you to "be still" and dare to spend some time in silence asking God to reveal himself to you.

Henri Nouwen wrote, "Solitude is the place of the great struggle and the great encounter—the struggle against the compulsions of the false self, and the encounter with the loving God who offers himself as the substance of the new self." If you seek an encounter with a fairy tale, your search will come up empty. But a wholehearted prayer for God to become real to you is a prayer that will always be answered.

How did you feel when you learned the truth about Santa Claus, the Easter Bunny, and the Tooth Fairy? What about how you felt when you discovered the truth about God?

How well do you like silence? When have you felt that God wanted you to wait and listen for his voice above all the noise in your life?

Read Zephaniah 3:17, Isaiah 41:10, and Psalm 33:11. When has God shown up in your life when you needed him most? In what difficult times have you wondered when (or even if) he would show up?

THE
BIGGEST
LIES

Tearing Off the False Nametags
That Cover Up Your True Identity

CHAPTER 6

CONFESSIONS OF A BURNED-OUT PREACHER'S KID

*This is the true perfection of a man,
to find out his own imperfections.*

ST. AUGUSTINE

Hello, my name is "Preacher's Kid." I am still in recovery for this. I spent roughly the first eighteen years of my life seated in the front row in the sanctuary of Hobson Road Community Church in Downers Grove, Illinois, next to my mom and two brothers. I suffered through more church potluck dinners than any human being should be forced to endure. Rumor has it the government once considered using the church potluck as a form of coercion to make terrorists and criminals spill the beans. If you saw some of the peculiar homemade dishes I've seen, you'd much sooner spill the beans than eat them.

I used to follow my mother in the potluck line after church in the family center whispering the question, "Who made this?" as I pointed to every dish on the table. This was an essential tool of survival for a preacher's kid. Especially since there was one lady in our church who possessed a deadly combination of passions: she believed she had been given the spiritual gift of hospitality, but she also owned about three thousand cats. To this day, I occasionally wake up in a cold sweat thanks to nightmares reminding me of the fateful day Dorothy (bless her heart) brought a wedding cake to church for a young couple who couldn't afford an expensive reception. I remember standing next to my mother as this kind lady was cutting giant slices of wedding cake and handing them out on plastic plates with plastic forks. Now, normally I would have known better and proceeded with caution, but this cake looked so delicious I guess I just got carried away.

I was only a few bites from polishing off the whole slice of cake when my mother complimented the baker, "What a beautiful cake!" Dorothy, with a deep sigh, responded, "Oh, thanks, but I was so mad this morning. The minute I finished the cake, those darn cats decided to jump up on the table in my kitchen and walk all over it." My mom, ever so hopeful, said, "Oh, that's too bad. You had to start all over and make a new cake?" Dorothy replied, "Oh, heavens no! But it took me forever to patch up all the holes in the frosting!" At that point, I threw up a little in my mouth and vowed to always do an in-depth investigation before allowing any piece of cake to touch my lips again. But at least now I can say I've tasted cat cake.

It wasn't just the potluck that left me a little burned out on church life, though. The pressure that came along with the title of "preacher's son" is what really got to me over time. Don't get me wrong. My dad and mom are incredible people, and knowing the circumstances many other kids have growing up, I would gladly choose my parents and my path if I had to do it all over again. But each childhood presents its own challenges, doesn't it? My counselor once jokingly said to me, "All parents wind up giving their kids one reason or another to need counseling later in life." Well, if it wasn't my parents, it was my parents' profession that provided me with spiritual hurdles I've had to jump over on my way to a healthy relationship with God and a healthy view of my identity.

MY *BRAVEHEART* REBELLION

My brothers and I had little ways of rebelling—you know, not upsetting the whole applecart, more like staging minor revolutions. We're not talking Custer's Last Stand, but maybe his second-to-last stand. The one that never made the papers. For example, one Sunday morning we thought it would be funny to climb under my dad's seat and roll the pant legs of his suit up so that when he stood up to preach, the church would think he forgot how to dress himself. He couldn't figure out why the entire congregation was snickering until he looked down to see his business socks making a surprise appearance.

Another favorite activity took place at the once-a-month church hymn sing. People could raise their hand and request a song out of the hymnal, and then the entire church would sing it together. We feverishly tore through the pages trying to find the most obscure hymn that we were sure nobody, not even the pianist, had ever heard. It was even better if we could find a song with a vaguely suggestive title that, if taken out of context, might have an entirely different meaning. My brothers and I would burst out laughing as we listened to the people stumble through four verses of "Amazing Grace's" lesser-known second cousin, "Breathe on Me." But my personal favorite was selecting "The Star-Spangled Banner." Did you know that is in church hymnals? If you want to see an awkward situation, watch a confused congregation sing our nation's anthem unexpectedly. A couple of people would stand. Others put a hand up to their heart. Still others would salute. It was like nobody knew what to do with their hands. We loved being the instigators of the most oddly patriotic moment of the monthly church hymn sing.

Of course, our pranks were all fun and games until we got sent to Dad's office. I'm not proud of what I'm about to tell you next. This was not my finest hour. But anyone who's ever felt the pressure to be perfect might understand why a good preacher's kid would finally stand up and say, "Enough!" Maybe it was the heat of that midsummer Wednesday night that got to me. I don't know.

Our parents, who were headed to their midweek church service, dropped off my peers and me at the little white house on the church's property. Our church had its own version of Boy Scouts called "Royal Rangers." Now, something you should know about me: I am not what you might call an outdoorsman.

I've grown to love nature in recent years, but only if I'm a short distance from a steak dinner. Being forced to stay in a hotel that doesn't provide at least a continental breakfast is my idea of "roughing it." Oh, the horror. What am I, an animal? As a kid, the thought of earning a badge for starting my own fire or setting up a tent in the woods was not high on my list of priorities. But when you're the preacher's kid, you go to Royal Rangers whether you like it or not. So I went.

Our troop leader liked to begin every meeting with prayer. Any guesses which boy he picked to pray every week? *Ding ding ding.* The preacher's kid! Every week I heard the leader say, "Matthew, go ahead and pray to start us off tonight," and without hesitation I would bow my head and toss up a quick prayer that I thought would meet his approval so we could get on with our exploration of the great outdoors (or at least the great backyard of the church). But on this particular Wednesday night, my response to his request for an opening prayer was different. "No," I blurted out. *Did I just say that?* I thought. The troop leader who had already bowed his head looked back up at me stunned and said, "Excuse me?" I fired back before there was time for second thoughts. "How come I'm the one who always has to pray? Why don't you ask one of the other kids?" The other boys' jaws were on the ground by this point. The troop leader's answer was gasoline on this little Royal Ranger's homemade bonfire. "Well, because you're the preacher's kid and you are supposed to set a good example for the rest of this group!" That was it. This was no longer a question of whether I really did or didn't want to pray. His words summed up the pressure I had felt for a long time, and my moment to step out from under the suffocating weight of "setting the example" had arrived. I might as well have been standing on top of a hill in Scotland wearing a bearskin cloak with my face covered in war paint and my sword drawn, because I was about to stand up for freedom in a way that would make William Wallace proud. This was my *Braveheart* rebellion. "I don't want to pray, and you can't make me!" I shouted. He then issued the ultimatum. I could either pray like a good preacher's kid or get kicked out of Royal Rangers and face the consequences. But I had already decided. There was no turning back.

I stood up and marched right out of Royal Rangers for the last time and made the long walk to Dad's office, convinced I would soon be grounded for the rest of my life. My dad didn't hand out any punishment that night. He must have known this was a potential turning point in my life. Would the pressure of being the preacher's kid push me away from God or would my heart remain soft and open to his plan for my life? My dad said something to me that I have never forgotten. "Son, if you look for God in other people, you'll find it sometimes, but people will inevitably let you down. And you will let them down. Nobody's perfect. But you can't let that affect your view of God. Keep your eyes on him. Aim to please him, and don't worry about trying to live up to everyone else's standards. You're human. God loves you, and I love you too." I know . . . pretty cool response from my preacher dad. A response I so desperately needed in that middle school moment.

HELLO, MY NAME IS
"PRETENDER"

There are good kinds of pressure. Like the pressure that produces diamonds. Deep within the earth, about a hundred miles below the surface, extreme heat and pressure push carbon atoms together to form these beautiful stones that hold great value. We all would love for the pressures we face every day to produce diamonds in our lives, but most of the time they don't. But we want people to see sparkly perfection in us, so we do everything we can to present the appearance of a diamond with no flaws. Our goal, then, becomes getting people to focus on the shine of an inauthentic life while we try our best to keep up. (By the way, an article at diamonds.net says that truly flawless diamonds are "nearly as scarce as unicorns.")

I know a man who bought his wife what she thought were beautiful diamond earrings for their anniversary. We're talking two carats in each ear. These were some major rocks. But the husband didn't tell his wife that while diamonds might be a girl's best friend, hers weren't real. They were made from the much less expensive imposter, cubic zirconia. Nevertheless, the wife couldn't tell the difference, and she showed off her new earrings wherever she went. Years later, when the couple was switching insurance companies, she was asked to get an appraisal on all of her expensive jewelry. It was only then that she discovered from the jeweler that her priceless diamonds weren't so priceless after all. I'm pretty sure that guy is still sleeping on the pullout couch in their living room.

For the person feeling pressure to be perfect, life can become more about appearance than reality. Did you know that it is possible to look and talk and act like a good Christian but be living with a heart in critical condition? The Bible describes this type of lifestyle by saying, "These people come near to me with their mouth and honor me with their lips, but their hearts are far from me" (Isaiah 29:13 NIV). This is the plight of a "professional Christian." That's what I am. That's what I've always been. From the son of a preacher to the singer of songs, I've lived out my entire spiritual journey in the public eye. And I have learned all the right buttons to push in order to make you think I'm doing all right.

This started back in the front row of church with my mom on Sunday mornings. I knew that if I raised my hand in worship during the slow song that the mother sitting behind me would elbow her son and say, "Why can't you be more like Matthew?" I knew that if I came to the altar for prayer after the Sunday service that people would see me and be impressed by the fact that I wasn't in a hurry to get to the post-service potluck (if they only knew). I memorized all the important Bible verses and could recite them on command. I had the "Christian" thing down. Still do. I know how to put the right words to the right melody. I know how to speak church-y language, the kind that will get everyone riled up and shouting a strong "Amen." If I wanted to, I could even write this chapter in such a way that would avoid revealing anything less than perfect about myself, thus addressing this topic of perfection from some falsely "vulnerable" place, and still escaping with my image unscathed. But keeping up the perception of perfection is exhausting.

When you realize perfection is impossible, you are left with the choice of two paths: The one that leads to coming clean and accepting the fact that you're a flawed human being. Or the one that leads to spending all of your time and energy working to keep up the appearance of spiritual perfection. Unfortunately, far too often I have found my feet wandering down that second path. What are some signs that you, too, might be a professional Christian? Well, how about a pop quiz? The comedian Jeff Foxworthy became famous for his "You might be a redneck if . . ." jokes. So let's play a little game called, "You might be a professional Christian if . . ."

You might be a professional Christian if . . . you pray the loudest in your small-group prayer circle, making sure everybody hears you.

You might be a professional Christian if . . . you post epic Instagram photos of your Bible laid open next to a morning cup of coffee with some clever caption like "A little bit of coffee and a whole lotta Jesus."

You might be a professional Christian if . . . you raise your hands in worship at the biggest part of "10,000 Reasons" just in case the cameraman at your megachurch puts you on the big screen.

The pressure comes from beyond the church too. Society adds to the pressure to display a perfect persona through social media posts on Facebook, Instagram, Twitter, Snapchat, and others. I can choose to post only the perfect pictures of my family on a beach vacation with everybody smiling and happy. Nobody has to know that we were all sweaty, annoyed, and fighting with each other seconds before that shot was taken. Thanks to social media, we can pick and choose which parts of our lives, our thoughts, our experiences we want to share with the world and then hide the rest away. Every day we are creating our own highlight reels. No need to expose a weakness when you've got the power to create the perfect image.

Mark Zuckerberg, founder of Facebook, described how people who use his site are "building an image and identity for themselves, which in a sense is their brand." We're all in the marketing business pushing our brand. The temptation to make our brand shine like a diamond makes fessing up about our flaws less and less of an option. We are the creators of our cubic zirconia public persona. It can get to the point where even the good things we do are driven by wrong motivations. We have to ask ourselves some tough, probing questions: "Am I reading my Bible because I want to grow in my faith and get closer to the heart of God? Or am I doing it so I can find a scripture to scribble in my journal and take an artsy picture to post online to present the *appearance* of someone who is close to the heart of God?" (Confession: I just did that this morning.) Jesus said, "Everything they do is done for people to see" (Matthew 23:5 NIV). And while the outlets we use to show the world our best sides might be high-tech these days, people have worn "Pretender" on their nametags ever since Adam and Eve were first finding creative uses for leaves.

The Bible tells us that some of the biggest pretenders in history were the teachers of the law and the Pharisees, the religious leaders. During Jesus's ministry on earth, his harshest warnings were not spoken to the prostitute or the tax collector or the drunk or the murderer, but to the pretender:

> Woe to you, teachers of the law and Pharisees, you hypocrites! You clean the outside of the cup and dish, but inside they are full of greed and self-indulgence. Woe to you, teachers of the law and Pharisees, you hypocrites! You are like whitewashed tombs, which look beautiful on the outside but on the inside are full of the bones of the dead . . . In the same way, on the outside you appear to people as righteous but on the inside you are full of hypocrisy and wickedness. (Matthew 23:25–28 NIV)

Jesus saw right through the artificial shine of the Pharisees' perfect perception and called out their hearts' true condition. In another verse he warned, "Watch out! Don't do your good deeds publicly, to be admired by others, for you will lose the reward from your Father in heaven" (Matthew 6:1). Jesus could have remained silent and let these pretenders go on pretending. But he spoke up in order to *wake up* the pretenders then and now. The Pharisees were missing the point and on the verge of missing the reward. And while his words for them might have been harsh, Jesus, the only perfect one who ever lived, was *freeing* them from the pressure to be perfect. I believe he wants to free you and me as well. He knows there are life-hindering side effects to becoming a pretender. Here are just a few that I've experienced firsthand in my own struggle with perfection.

Isolation

Pretenders have to protect that perfect image at all costs. But this makes it hard to be around other people. As a result, pretenders prefer isolation over community and accountability. Pretenders would rather withdraw from meaningful relationships than be vulnerable with the messier parts of their lives.

Unfair Expectations of Others

Pretenders tend to live like the Pharisees did, projecting their own standards of perfection on other people. Pretenders tend to judge others more harshly and compare themselves favorably to others, almost enjoying seeing others fall or fail morally, praying like the Pharisee who "stood by himself and prayed this prayer: 'I thank you, God, that I am not like other people—cheaters, sinners, adulterers. I'm certainly not like that tax collector!'" (Luke 18:11). Notice Scripture highlights that the Pharisee was by himself, isolated.

Spiritual Lifelessness

Jesus described pretenders as "whitewashed tombs," beautiful on the outside but carrying the bones of the dead on the inside. Pretenders' motivation has shifted from pleasing God to pleasing man. The act of worship becomes a performance while the lines of real, genuine communication with God are cut. Scripture study is for show, not for growth. In the book of Revelation, God warns the church in Laodicea, "I know all the things you do, that you are neither hot nor cold. I wish that you were one or the other! But since you are like lukewarm water, neither hot nor cold, I will spit you out of my mouth!" (3:15–16). The pretender has lost his heat, and has settled for a lukewarm spiritual existence.

Missed Impact in the World

The world won't be changed by encounters with pretenders. There's nothing magnetic about professional Christians. Ironically, the Pharisees and teachers of the law actually thought they were doing God's work. But how can God really use you if you aren't really you? Scripture highlights not the ministry of those who were pretending, but instead the flawed servants of God who did great things. David, Samson, Paul, Moses, and the list goes on. An imperfect world needs to see imperfect people pointing to a perfect God.

HELLO, MY NAME IS "REAL"

The discovery of who I am is an equal discovery of who I am not. And one of the things I can say with great certainty is that I am not perfect. No one is. No one but Jesus. "This High Priest of ours understands our weaknesses, for he faced all of the same testings we do, yet he did not sin" (Hebrews 4:15). This scripture is more than just information. This verse is an invitation! An invitation to take a deep, deep breath and let the pressure to be perfect roll off your shoulders once and for all. He "understands our weaknesses." As in my case, maybe you have also felt that pressure, and maybe for many years. Forget the pressure placed on you by church, family, social circles, or social media. Your perfect Savior knows that you're anything *but* perfect—and he loves you anyway. There is no more need to pretend. This is the starting line of an authentic Christian life.

Paul was no pretender. "Christ Jesus came into the world to save sinners—of whom I am the worst" (1 Timothy 1:15 NIV). These words can only be spoken from someone with a willingness to be real and a deep understanding of God's grace. Paul wasn't concerned about making people think he was perfect. In fact, he was the first to highlight the opposite, saying, "I will boast all the more gladly about my weaknesses, so that Christ's power may rest on me" (2 Corinthians 12:9 NIV). Instead of pretending, he was saying, "I'm a work in progress. I'm a mess! But look and see how God has changed my life." And Paul knew that by being real he would himself become a real example to others. "I was shown mercy so that in me, the worst of sinners, Christ Jesus might display his immense patience as an example for those who would believe in him and receive eternal life" (1 Timothy 1:16 NIV).

When we are willing to be the real, authentic, flawed diamonds we were created to be, God's power and patience go on display for others. And that's far more beautiful and cherished than living as cubic zirconium. Brennan Manning wrote in *The Ragamuffin Gospel*, "To live by grace means to acknowledge my whole life story, the light side and the dark. In admitting my shadow side I learn who I am and what God's grace means." By grace, Paul had been set free from any pressure to hide or deny his imperfections. In fact, he was actually empowered by his imperfections to speak more boldly about what God had done in his life. By acknowledging his dark side, he was opening the door for God to use every part of his story.

We pretenders prefer to decide for God which parts of our stories he can use. We build our highlight reels and then offer up all of our good stuff, saying, "Here you go, God. Use me." But what if all the while God is looking back at us, saying, *I know about your good stuff. I'm the one who gave it to you. Now hand over all the rest. Give me your strongest temptation, your Achilles' heel. Give me your shadow side you're afraid to show. Give me the worst parts of your life, the roughest corners of your character. Dare to believe that I see it all and love you still. Dare to believe that I can shine brighter through a real sinner than a perfect pretender.*

So, what's it gonna be? Will you allow the pressure to be perfect turn you into a pretender? Or will you be one of the few brave souls who dares to be the truest, most rough-around-the-edges, far-from-perfect, authentic version of you? Grace's strong arms have lifted the pressure of perfection off of your shoulders. You're free now to tell the whole story.

How is it possible to look and talk and act like a good Christian but live with a heart in critical condition? Have you ever grown tired (or become burned out) by portraying a perfect life?

What "You might be a professional Christian if . . ." jokes can you come up with, based on your personal experience?

Read 2 Corinthians 12:9 and 1 Timothy 1:16. When we are willing to be real, revealing the good and bad within us, how does God use us to reveal himself to others?

CHAPTER 7

A CASE OF MISTAKEN IDENTITY

It ain't what they call you, it's what you answer to.

W. C. FIELDS

According to a recent article published by the American Psychological Association, titled "Mistaken Identity," 305 people who were once wrongfully convicted of crimes in the past two decades have been set free thanks to DNA evidence (apa.org). An organization called the Innocence Project helped exonerate 170 of those people, all of whom spent years or even decades in prison before the truth was discovered. Try to imagine such a horribly sudden change of events taking place in someone's life. One day you're doing your thing, going to work, stopping at the grocery store, enjoying a meal with your family. And the next day you're hearing the haunting crack of a judge's gavel slamming down in a courtroom declaring you guilty of a crime you didn't commit. William Dillon knows what that's like. Just days before he was supposed to try out as a pitcher for the Detroit Tigers in 1981, this future major leaguer was arrested on murder charges. He spent twenty-seven years behind bars until DNA evidence exonerated him and ultimately set him free. In his midfifties now, he missed his chance to see his baseball dream come true.

Now check out this statistic: approximately three-quarters of those wrongful convictions involved false eyewitness testimony. In other words, hundreds of people have been put behind bars simply because someone incorrectly identified them as the guilty criminal. They pinned it on the wrong person, and the wrong person wound up behind bars. In the legal system, an eyewitness's testimony and opinion carry weight. And if that eyewitness is wrong, it can unfairly seal an innocent person's undeserved fate for life.

But the dangers of mistaken identity extend far beyond the legal system and into the matters of the heart as well. Jennifer knows what it's like to be falsely identified. This is an excerpt from the letter she wrote to me about her mistaken identity:

Your parents are supposed to tell you how much they love you. I grew up with constant criticism: "You're ugly. You're stupid. You're worthless. You're not good enough for anything. You are useless." You can only hear things like that for so long before you start believing them . . . Even to this day, I struggle with thinking I am not good enough in any aspect of my life . . . The tape in my mind keeps rewinding automatically and playing over and over again. I wish I could erase it.

These eyewitnesses in Jennifer's life, her parents, got it wrong. And the weight of their damaging words at such a young age threatened to sentence her to a life of emotional imprisonment. Her nametag had been filled in for her from the time she was a child. Those damaging words—*ugly, useless, stupid, worthless*—were hatefully scribbled in by people who failed to see her true identity, and for a long time that mistaken eyewitness testimony held her captive. "You can only hear things like that for so long before you start to believe them."

Even as I write this, a news story just popped up on my phone that is such a sad and vivid example of how damaging cases of mistaken identity can be. The parents of a four-year-old girl were arrested and brought into custody in Arkansas after social workers were made aware of and reported evidence of abuse taking place. When the child was rescued, police said she had been abused so badly that she had a black eye, dried blood in the corners of her mouth, and deep purple bruises all over her body. But it's what she said when a social worker asked her name that was truly startling. "Idiot," she whispered. Police say that she had been called "idiot" so often and for so long, that was the first word that sprung into her young mind. Mistaken identity. Because of her parents' evil actions and wounding words, a precious little girl thinks her name is actually "Idiot." She will undoubtedly have to spend years of her life dealing with the psychological and emotional trauma caused by her parents.

Has your nametag ever been filled in with damaging words used by people to mistakenly identify you? Maybe you have been a victim of bullying at school, or found yourself repeatedly on the receiving end of hurtful and demeaning words spoken by a spouse. Perhaps you've been criticized by a coworker or insulted by a coach. Maybe Jennifer's story or that little girl's hit you hard because you, too, have been crushed by careless criticism of a parent or even abused at a young age. We love little clichés like, "Sticks and stones may break my bones, but words can never hurt me," but at best, that little sentiment is wishful thinking. Damaging words do serious damage to the soul, no matter how young or old you are. What people say about you carries weight. Words change the way you see yourself when you look in the mirror. They alter the way you carry yourself when you go out in public. All it takes is one criticism, one cut down, or one time being the butt of everyone else's joke to steal your confidence and replace it with insecurity that will ruin your life if you let it.

The world goes out of its way to make you believe you are not good enough, pretty enough, skinny enough, smart enough, athletic enough, rich enough, popular enough, qualified enough. Just. Not. Enough. Behind every false eyewitness's damaging words is the same enemy whom the Bible describes as the father of lies (John 8:44). His goal is simple: to replay those words over and over in your mind until, ultimately, you give up hope that you could be anything other than what the world has said about you. He will try to use the voices around you to drown out the still, small voice of the one who made you. Satan knows that if he can get you to believe a lie about who you are, then there's a good chance you'll never become who you were meant to be, who God created you to be.

THE KING OF DAIRY QUEEN

If our hearts were gardens, I think we'd remember the first time certain seeds were planted there. Especially seeds of insecurity. I know mine remembers the moment the first seeds of insecurity were planted on impressionable soil. I remember the day I learned that my first name rhymed with another word that wasn't quite the flattering description a fourth-grade kid would want to be associated with. I heard a few of the kids at school intentionally inserting my name into that playground refrain. "Matt-Matt-bo-bat banana-fanna-fo-fat!" They knew what they were doing too. And they did it over and over. I got a new nametag that day, and I never looked in the mirror the same way again. My struggle with self-image continued and only increased as I made my way through junior high, high school, college, and even to this day.

I was overweight as a child, but I never really thought of it that way until those kids pointed it out the way only kids can do. I mean, I do recall wondering why all of my clothes throughout elementary school had a "Husky" tag inside. I played youth-league football and dreamed of being the quarterback or the running back—you know, one of the fun positions—but any kid over a certain weight had a black piece of tape put on the back of his helmet, and they were relegated to the offensive line. No fun. Now, I don't want to blame my parents entirely for the fact that I struggled with my weight as a kid, but looking back, I do see some patterns that certainly did not help me to learn a healthy lifestyle. The main culprit keeping the baby fat attached to me was a magical place called Dairy Queen. Dilly Bars, Peanut Buster Parfaits, Blizzards. Uh, yes, yes, and YES! For some families, a place like DQ might only be designated for special occasions. But a typical Tuesday was special enough for my family to indulge in frozen treats. And to make matters worse, there was one located just a couple of miles from our little yellow house on Janes Avenue in Downers Grove, Illinois.

Now, my dad's idea of exercise when I was growing up was for us to take a bike ride. Yet, mysteriously, that bike ride would always seem to end at the same location: Dairy Queen. Whatever calories we burned off on the way were more than made up for as we polished off our ice cream. Then, after our tummies were full, we couldn't be expected to pedal all the way home. So we called my mom for a ride home. She would pick us up, we would throw our bikes in the backseat and lazily be driven back to the house. After all, I'm pretty sure you're supposed to wait *at least* thirty minutes after eating ice cream before getting on a bicycle, right? Or maybe that's swimming. Well, don't do that either.

It wasn't just the sweets that got me in trouble, though. I grew up in the generation that lived at the corner of Super-Size and Get-Your-Money's-Worth. All the fast food restaurants had begun offering the option to "super-size" your value meal. For just a dollar more, you could upgrade to the ginormous cup of soda *and* extra-large order of salty French fries. And just in case you finished your barrel-sized drink, they were now also offering *free refills*! Now, this is where my dad comes in again. He always made sure we got the full "value" from every value meal. I remember one conversation with my dad at the end of a meal at McDonald's.

Dad: Son, why don't you go get a free refill before we leave?
Me: I'm not thirsty anymore.
Dad: But it's *free*.
Me: Yeah, but I'm full. I don't need any more.
Dad: Son, I don't think you understand. It's FREE. Why would you *not* get one?
Me: Okay Dad. I'll fill it up.

Perhaps that was my dad's way of sticking it to the man. Looking back, I wonder if he was trying to drink enough Diet Coke to make up for all the taxes he was paying Uncle Sam. We get a pretty good laugh about that now every time we find ourselves both standing at a fountain drink machine. And to this day, Dad always gets his free refill.

Early in my career, I was driving myself from small town to small town playing even smaller concerts. I remember being booked to play a show in a tiny Illinois town one summer. I arrived early to that one-stoplight town and happened to notice a Dairy Queen. So I pulled into the drive-through line. I heard a girl's voice through the speaker, "Welcome to Dairy

Queen. May I take your order?" Why, yes, you can! I ordered a Butterfinger Blizzard (because that's exactly what you need just before getting up on stage to sing). When I arrived at the pick-up window, the girl who had taken my order was blowing pink bubbles with her chewing gum as she took my money from my hand. She made eye contact with me, and then she looked over at something on the wall in the restaurant. Then she looked back at me again, and then back at the wall. Turns out, there was a poster with my picture on it, advertising my show that night. She blew another bubble and then asked, "That you on that poster?" Enjoying the fact that I had just been recognized, I smiled and said, "Yes. Yes, it is." She blew another bubble and then said, "Huh. You look a lot chubbier in person," just as she placed the large Blizzard in my hands. Stunned by both her comment and the irony of the moment as she was handing me a thousand calories of lactose, I handed the frozen goodness right back to her and said, "Thank you very much." Then I drove off. And guess what was ringing in my ears all the way to the show? "MATT-MATT-BO-BAT BANANA-FANNA-FO-FAT."

HELLO, MY NAME IS "INSECURE"

If I'm being honest, I've felt this deep need for approval and affirmation for as long as I can remember. I wonder if that started back on the playground when my eyes were opened to see that from someone else's opinion, that false eyewitness, I was in some way flawed. From my childhood to this very day, moments of insecurity have at times paralyzed me.

Why did I vote for myself for homecoming king? Why did it matter? Why did it feel so good to win? Why did I need the popularity? Why have I craved the applause of people all these years? Why am I writing this book? Why do I hope you like it? Why do I need you to like it? Why am I afraid you won't?

Sometimes insecurity will hit me just before I walk on stage for a concert. All of a sudden I will be convinced that I'm not wearing the right shirt. So I'll hurry and try on another. Then another, and another. By this point, I am feeling fully flustered and stressed out over a stupid shirt, my mind a million miles away from focusing on what matters—the chance to minister to people through song. My wife is usually with me on the tour bus before I walk on stage, and I thank God for her. I'll ask her over and over again, "Should I wear this? Or this? Or this?" Finally, she will calm me down and say, "Matthew, you look great. And those six shirts you just tried on are all the same color anyway. It doesn't matter."

Reading what I just wrote, I'm afraid you might be thinking, *Wow, this guy's got issues!* But I guess that's part of what this book is about, putting myself out there. Because here's the thing . . . As much as I hope you won't settle for the name "Insecure," I don't want to feel that insecurity anymore either. I don't want to let it maintain its grip on my mind. I don't want it to matter whether or not I receive a crowd's applause. I don't think God wants that for me either. In fact, I know that's not his will for me. "My dear friends, don't let public opinion influence how you live out our glorious, Christ-originated faith" (James 2:1 MSG).

I want to write music, sing songs, write books, and live my life free from the opinions of other people once and for all. I love the children's story *The Velveteen Rabbit*. There is a conversation between the horse and the rabbit, two stuffed animals, about what it's like to be real. The horse is educating the rabbit, saying, "Generally, by the time you are Real, most of your hair has been loved off, and your eyes drop out and you get loose in your joints and very shabby. But these things don't matter at all, because once you are Real you can't be ugly, except to people who don't understand." Oh, to be that kind of real, secure enough to ignore the false eyewitnesses who "don't understand." But how?

OUR SPIRITUAL DNA

God offers us a way to fend off the firepower of the false eyewitnesses around us and inform Insecurity that it has spent its last day dominating our identities. "For though we live in the world, we do not wage war as the world does. The weapons we fight with are not the weapons of the world. On the contrary, they have divine power to demolish strongholds. We demolish arguments and every pretension that sets itself up against the *knowledge of God*, and we *take captive every thought* to make it obedient to Christ" (2 Corinthians 10:3–5 NIV, emphasis mine). Knowledge is our weapon. But not just any knowledge. Our "knowledge of God" is what gives us the power to turn the tables and take captive every lie and every thought that tries to keep us locked up. There is power in knowing and believing who God is. And there is power in learning and receiving who God says we are. I bet he knew we'd need more than one reminder.

You are created in his image. For starters, God your creator says he created you "in his own image" (Genesis 1:27 NIV).

You belong. "My dear children, you come from God and belong to God" (1 John 4:4 MSG).

You are chosen as God's special possession. "But you are a chosen people, a royal priesthood, a holy nation, God's special possession" (1 Peter 2:9 NIV).

You are a masterpiece. "For we are God's masterpiece" (Ephesians 2:10).

You are his child. "For you are all children of God through faith in Christ Jesus" (Galatians 3:26).

I think it's safe to say you're kind of a big deal to God. He never once looks at you, his creation, with regret or with thoughts of what he would do differently if he could start you over again. You are who God says you are. Now, remember how I mentioned that 305 people who have been wrongfully convicted through our legal system have been set free? Remember what eventually exonerated them? DNA evidence. In crime investigations, DNA is as good as fact. DNA is proof. DNA replaces hearsay with certainty. DNA trumps some eyewitnesses' pointing finger every time. And just as we each have a physical DNA, God's Word informs us of our spiritual DNA as well. DNA can be found in a fingerprint or even a strand of hair. So, who better to inform you of your spiritual DNA than the one who knows you "down to the last detail—even numbering the hairs on your head" (Matthew 10:30 MSG)? When we flood our hearts and minds daily with these reminders from Scripture of our spiritual DNA, we can ensure that the enemy's false eyewitness testimony has no power to keep us behind bars.

I love David's words in Psalm 139:14: "I praise you because I am fearfully and wonderfully made; your works are wonderful, I know that full well" (NIV). To know something "full well" means to know without a doubt. That's what knowledge of your spiritual DNA will do for you. It will remove all doubt that you are anything or anyone other than who God says you are. And in the absence of doubt, confidence grows. That's what has happened with my friend Jennifer, whose story I shared at the beginning of this chapter.

If her story sounded familiar, it's probably because you read it in a book I previously published. In that book on forgiveness, I wrote about how "Melissa" was learning to forgive those false eyewitnesses in her life who made her feel "ugly," "worthless," "stupid." Since she was still struggling with this part of her life, and her relationship with her family was strained, Jennifer didn't feel comfortable using her real name. She later reached out to me again, saying she had changed her mind. She wanted me to use her real name because it was time to step out from the shadows of that low self-esteem once and for all, but by then it was too late—the book had already been printed and being shipped around the country.

I usually don't make a habit of telling the same story twice, but I thought I'd make an exception so that Jennifer could see her real name and because I believe it could help you begin to see yours.

Jennifer, wherever you are, I want you to know how proud I am of you for finding your real name. For daring to believe that those false eyewitnesses who hurt you do not get to decide your identity for you. You know you are so much more. You are a mother, a wife, a friend, and a chosen child of God. You have discovered your spiritual DNA, and you are no longer held captive by the mistaken identity that once imprisoned you. You've even inspired this singer, who's tired of trying on so many shirts, to tear up the nametag that says "Insecure" once and for all and to walk in the confidence that I am fearfully and wonderfully made. Like you, I can finally say I know that "full well."

When have you been labeled with a false name? How hard was it not to own it, or to get rid of it?

How does your "spiritual DNA" help you stop believing the lies about who you are and start believing the truth of who God says you are?

Read Psalm 139:14. What are the signs that you have been "fearfully and wonderfully made"? And how can you know "full well" his works are wonderful?

CHAPTER 8

STUMBLING BLOCKS OR STEPPING STONES

You intended to harm me,
but God intended it all for good.
GENESIS 50:20

In recent years, I have surprisingly taken quite a liking to hiking. The rhyme in that last sentence was completely intentional. There are people who just look as though they were made for the outdoors, aren't there? Like my friend Derek, who is some kind of a superhero yet to be imagined by Stan Lee. He's a skilled hiker, skier, mountain biker, *and* worship leader at his church in the mountains. He's got the chiseled jawline and a percentage of body fat that rivals skim milk. This guy is a lean, mean, worship-leading machine. Then there's me. A low-altitude-dwelling, guitar-playing city boy who's never been described with the terms *rugged* or *skilled outdoorsman*.

I recently returned from a trip to Colorado, and thanks to some beautiful late-spring weather, I was able to hit several trails and explore some of the most beautiful surroundings anyone could lay eyes on. But even before I headed to the mountains, I made a visit to REI and bought pretty much everything they had to offer. I swear that salesperson spotted this rookie the moment I opened my car door. I left that store with hiking boots, a backpack, a water bottle, an all-weather zip-up hoodie, and a half dozen other hiking-related items I was told I might need. I was prepared for anything that could potentially come my way once I ventured into the wild. Well, almost anything. I found out quickly that a trip to REI doesn't make a person any more of a skilled outdoorsman than a round of Putt-Putt makes someone ready for the PGA Tour.

Derek served as my guide for a few hikes, and we had a great time talking along the way. Of course, he was the only one able to talk. I was too busy fighting to catch my breath. If you've ever traveled to higher elevation, you know that the act of breathing quickly transitions from something you do without even thinking about into something you are quite aware of with very labored and focused huffing and puffing. After feeling sorry for slowing my superhero-worship-leader friend down, I decided to venture out on my own one morning. There was one particular peak that I had set my sights on, and I had made up my mind that I would keep hiking until I reached the top. This was a bad idea. I had a book that described all of the trails in the area where I was staying (thanks again, REI), which categorized the difficulty of this particular trail as "hard." I was sure that simply meant it would be hard for children or for those who forgot to buy all the stuff I bought at the store. Either way, when I decide I'm going to do something, not even an extreme shortage of oxygen can stop me. Besides, I was told by the locals that the view at the top was definitely worth the climb.

Just minutes into my hike, I realized why this trail was designated as "hard." The incline was steep, covering an elevation of three thousand feet in a very short distance. I kept thinking, *I'm sure this will level out any minute and spill me into a nice meadow where I can catch my breath.* No luck, and no meadow. Just as I was getting in the zone and finding my stride up the side of the mountain, I heard a noise behind me getting closer by the minute. I tried to stay focused, keeping my eyes looking ahead. Was it a bear? A mountain lion? Was this how I was going to die? All of a sudden I heard a sweet little voice say, "Excuse me, coming through." Sure enough, I turned around to see an older woman, no younger than seventy-five, asking me to step aside so she and her little white poodle—yes, that's right, a tiny lap dog—could pass me on their way to the top of that "hard" trail. How's that for discouraging? The lady and her poodle passed me by in what seemed like a blaze of white lightning. Either that, or I was a lot more out of shape than I realized. This was one hike I would not be mentioning to my superhero-worship-leader-hiker friend.

So maybe I wasn't going to win the race against the lady and her dog, but I remained determined to reach that summit. Looking at the trail in front of me, I searched for rocks and little ledges solid enough for me to hoist myself up and cover more ground at a faster rate. I took advantage of anything and everything I could find useful. At one point I noticed beside the trail a tree with roots that had been exposed. These roots formed sort of a natural stairway in that particular section of the trail. The only problem was, I noticed the roots too late. My foot got caught and I fell, breaking my fall with my hands in the dirt. After picking myself up, dusting myself off, and making sure there weren't any old ladies or poodles mocking me, I resumed my hike. Only this time, instead of tripping over the roots, I was able to use them to my advantage as I made my way up the side of the mountain.

WILL YOU TRIP UP OR CLIMB ON?

We all have roots. A place we come from, a home we grew up in, a family we belong to. Our last names represent our roots for better or sometimes for worse. Some people look back over the course of their lives and see strong, healthy roots that have helped them flourish in life. But every family tree has its share of broken branches. And many of us have found some of our roots to be more an obstacle to overcome than a strong foundation to propel us to greater heights. Roots that trip us up can even be handed down through generations, causing a cycle of dysfunction that leaves one saying, "It runs in the family." What runs in your family? Alcoholism? Abuse? Divorce? Mental illness? Anger? Grudges? Just like the roots I encountered on my hike, our roots in life can either trip us up or lift us up.

There were some messed-up families in the Bible. We can't even get past the first four chapters of Genesis without Adam and Eve sinning against God and their son Cain killing his brother, Abel. A little further into that same book, we learn about a guy named Joseph and the incredibly dysfunctional family that threatened to ruin his life. Joseph's brother's hated him and wouldn't even speak to him. One day his brothers saw him coming toward them and said to each other, "Here comes that dreamer. Let's kill him and throw him into one of these old cisterns; we can say that a vicious animal ate him up. We'll see what his dreams amount to" (Genesis 37:19–20 MSG). Then, after having second thoughts, they decided to merely sell him as a slave. With brothers like that, who needs enemies?

Scripture says multiple times during the story of his life that even though his family had betrayed him, "The LORD was with Joseph" (39:2). As a result, Joseph was able to endure the hatred from his brothers, slavery, and even years in jail. In time he earned great respect from Pharaoh, who decided to place Joseph in charge of the entire country of Egypt. Talk about rags to riches! Joseph had gone from a coat of many colors torn to shreds to a seat of great responsibility over the entire country. He also rose above resentment when a severe famine left the people starving and Joseph's brothers traveled to Egypt for food. Little did they know their brother would decide their fate.

Joseph was overcome with emotion during their unexpected reunion. "Deeply moved . . . and about to burst into tears, Joseph hurried out into another room and had a good cry" (43:30 MSG). Seeing his brothers after all those years brought to the surface so much hurt from their betrayal, but in that moment, any anger or resentment he felt toward his brothers was outweighed by the realization that God had led him to this full-circle moment of redemption. Instead of returning hatred with hatred, Joseph told his brothers, "You intended to harm me, but God intended it all for good" (50:20).

Joseph was miraculously able to extend grace to the very people who tried to ruin his life. His brothers had given him the names "Unwanted," "Slave," "Abandoned," "Prisoner." But when we gain the power of perspective, our enemies immediately lose the power to control our identities. Joseph understood that even those who hurt him were just characters in God's bigger plan for his story. They weren't stumbling blocks. They were stepping stones, a stairway that led him to where God wanted him to be.

HELLO, MY NAME IS "WOUNDED"

Parents are supposed to protect their children from harm. They are supposed to be the open arms their kids can run into, knowing that they will be kept safe. But Kathy's parents were the very source of her deepest pain. If I were to sum up her life in one word, sadly I'd have to use the word *wounded*.

Kathy was the victim of horrible and unthinkable abuse at the hands of her parents. Severe physical and sexual abuse left a little girl shell-shocked and frightened of the world inside her own home and desperate to find a way out. At age thirteen, Kathy ran away from the home that hurt her so deeply in search of any open arms that would protect her. She was picked up while hitchhiking by a man who promised to do just that. He was a liar and his intentions were evil, and for the next several years of Kathy's life, she was held against her will as a victim of human trafficking. If there had been the slightest light of innocence flickering somewhere in a corner of her heart, it was snuffed out by a darkness we'd rather pretend doesn't exist in the world. The men who held her against her will introduced her to drugs, and she became heavily addicted as days turned to weeks, weeks to months, and months to years. Kathy was past the point of broken, and had long lost any hope of being saved.

A local ministry started by a woman who had once been in a similarly desperate, drug-addicted stage of life was on a mission to bravely reach into the dark corners of the community where Kathy was living in an attempt to rescue women from slavery. They found out about Kathy, and she became their mission. The problem was, after so many years of abuse and addiction, Kathy didn't even know there was a different way of life. I suppose a person can spend so many days in darkness that you forget what light looks like. Still, they were relentless in their pursuit of her and were finally able to bring her to safety. Her long journey toward physical, emotional, and spiritual healing had begun.

Moved by her story, I traveled to meet Kathy with a good friend from a local radio station that had been helping her get back on her feet. She greeted me at the front door of her one-bedroom apartment with a southern accent and a smile. She introduced me to her cat. Kathy was funny. I mean *really* funny. She had me laughing almost the whole time we were together. I brought my guitar, pulled it out, and asked if I could sing for her. I sang some hymns, took some requests, anything that might make her smile. At one point during my singing, I looked next to me and saw Kathy crying the kind of tears that fall as if they've been held back for years. I stopped singing and said, "Kathy, I'm sorry. I didn't mean to make you cry."

She responded, "No, it's a good thing. You see, for most of my life I had mentally and emotionally removed myself from my own body. It was like I was outside of myself looking in. I did it so I wouldn't feel the pain anymore. I thought I'd never be able to cry again. So, now when I cry, it tells me that I'm feeling something again. It's a good thing. Just keep on singin'."

Life did a number on Kathy. Her roots made for a broken road filled with one stumbling block after the other. She had been broken down to nothing. But there she was that afternoon seated right beside me, and with every tear that rolled down her cheek, I saw a broken person rising from the rubble of a demolished life, smiling at the thought of how good it felt. Just as with Joseph, she was having a "good cry," the kind of cry that says it's okay to feel again. Your roots can't hurt you anymore. They've made you stumble for the last time. It's time to start climbing again. It's time to start feeling again.

I SEE MENDED

Unlike Joseph, who saw his story come full circle, Kathy's story has yet to reach its full redemption. At the moment I am writing this, I am staring at a plaque I had made with her name on it that holds handwritten lyrics to a song I wrote for her after leaving her apartment that afternoon. The song is called "Mended," and I had planned to deliver the plaque to her as a special surprise and to have her be the first person to hear the song inspired by her life. But Kathy is very sick, both physically and psychologically. When I excitedly called my friend from the radio station to tell her I was coming to town to surprise Kathy, I was informed that she had disappeared and nobody could find her. That plaque honoring Kathy still sits on the floor of my music room in the hopes that I will one day be able to place it in her hands.

I wish I could have written a much different ending to this chapter. Oh, how I wish every broken story could be neatly pieced back together the way it should be in a nice Christian book from a nice Christian singer. But this is real life. And real life takes time. Real life has nasty, ugly roots that rise up from the dirt path we're traveling on, threatening to trip us up at every turn. Real life has detours and setbacks and relapses. Even Joseph was not immune to old feelings of anger toward his family, which had hurt him so deeply. But ultimately he was able to see that God intended everything for Joseph's good. In other words, God never left Joseph. And God has never left Kathy, wherever she is right now.

Perhaps you can relate in some way to the stories of Joseph and Kathy. Perhaps you, too, have been deeply wounded by those who were supposed to keep you safe. Just as God was with Joseph, God is with Kathy. And just as God is with Kathy, he is with you too. Real life is no match for a real God who has real plans for your life. No roots, no matter how deep in the ground, have the power to stop what God is going to do with you. You may not be able to see it yet, but God's not finished. In this moment, you might look in the mirror and see someone wounded by roots that have tripped you up for too long. Or you might look at someone else's life and think, *There's no good that could possibly come from their situation.* But your heavenly Father draws full circles with our lives, working all things for the good, and "He heals the brokenhearted and bandages their wounds" (Psalms 147:3). We might see *wounded.* But rest assured, he sees *mended.*

When people or circumstances trip you up, how does God give you the strength and grace to claim the name "Victor" rather than "Victim"?

What circumstances in life have tripped you up? Which ones have you been able to use as stepping stones?

Read Genesis 50:20. Everyone likes a happy ending, but when stories don't go the way we want them to go, how can we keep our faith along the rough and rocky path?

CHAPTER 9

IDENTITY THEFT

Someone stole my mood ring.
I'm not sure how that makes me feel.
ANONYMOUS

I spend a good part of every year traveling around the country. As a result, I receive a call almost once a month from my bank inquiring about "suspicious" activity on my check card or credit card. A monthly statement of mine might read more like a travel itinerary for a contestant on *The Amazing Race*. Deodorant and a toothbrush might be purchased at a Walgreens in Boise, donuts and coffee from a local spot in Portland, and sushi from Pike Place Market in Seattle—all in the span of just one week-end on the road. One time my card was declined at a store in Springfield, Missouri, preventing me from making a purchase. So I called the credit card company to find out the reason. The representative on the other end of the phone asked, "Are you in South Africa right now?" "Uh, no. I've never even been to

South Africa. Why?" I replied. "Well, our records of your recent activity show that you just made a purchase at a department store in South Africa." Apparently my identity had been stolen somehow, and someone was using *my* name and *my* money to buy *their* things over eight thousand miles away. Thankfully, the representative on the phone was able to stop the card from being charged and send me a new one, taking the power away from that identity thief.

Having my identity stolen even for a day left me feeling powerless and unsettled. It was strange to think that somewhere in the world, someone held the keys to my life and could use them to unlock whatever doors they wanted. One in four people are victims of this kind of identity theft, where thieves pretend to be you to take over or open new accounts, file fake tax returns, rent or buy properties, or do other criminal things in your name. Companies like LifeLock are dedicated to helping people protect themselves from financial identity theft. Their job is to know all about how these identity thieves operate in order to better help their customers protect themselves.

While one out of four might be victims of financial identity theft, four out of four people are at risk of a different, much worse kind of identity theft. In every life, at every turn, Satan is trying to steal our spiritual identities. He wants nothing more than to victimize us by taking away our identity as chosen children of God. His goal is to take the keys to *our* life and control us until we find ourselves doing things we thought we would never do, saying things we thought we would never say, and living a life we thought we would never live.

Just as LifeLock focuses on knowing how identity thieves operate, it is essential that we know all we can about the enemy we are dealing with. The more we know, the better protected we can be from the devil's tricks and tactics. The ancient Chinese general and author of *The Art of War*, Sun Tzu, warned,

> If you know the enemy and know yourself, you need not fear the result of a hundred battles. If you know yourself but not the enemy, for every victory gained you will also suffer defeat. If you know neither the enemy nor yourself, you will succumb in every battle.

Protecting your identity is a battle. And in this battle, knowledge is power. You must know your enemy. You must know yourself. And you must know the truth.

HIS NAME IS . . .

God loves us too much to leave us guessing what kind of enemy we are up against. The Bible issues one warning after another of what kind of adversary we face in Satan. Here are some of the names given to Satan in Scripture:

- Father of lies (John 8:44)
- Serpent (Genesis 3:1)
- Roaring lion (1 Peter 5:8)
- Enemy (Matthew 13:39)
- Evil One (John 17:15)
- Deceiver (Revelation 12:9)

- Accuser (Revelation 12:10)
- Thief (John 10:10)

Each description of Satan gives even clearer insight into his destructive intentions with our lives. John 10:10 reveals Satan's simple, three-step plan to take you down and steal your identity. "The thief's purpose is to *steal* and *kill* and *destroy*" (emphasis mine). Notice the word *and* featured in that scripture. In other words, Satan won't be content with accomplishing only one or two of these three items on his agenda. He wants to . . .

Steal—A thief does not ask permission. A thief takes what belongs to someone else, most times striking when the victim least expects it. Your identity is something that he has no claim over, but he wants it and will attempt to steal it at a moment's notice.

And . . .

Kill—He wants to kill your dreams, your hopes, your ambitions, your innocence, your confidence. He won't stop coming at you until there are no longer any signs of spiritual life.

And . . .

Destroy—Satan will not settle for simply making a mess of your life. He will not stop until you are brought completely to your knees. He wants to obliterate your reputation, your family, your children, your health, and your life, leaving you a million miles from where God intended you to be.

When a sports team plans for an upcoming game, the coaching staff will provide players with a scouting report that they use as a study guide in their preparation for the contest. Historically, some of the most successful competitors are the ones who have been known to spend the most time studying their scouting reports and, as a result, seemingly anticipating their competition's every move before the game even begins. The Bible has given us a scouting report so that we won't be caught by surprise when Satan comes at us. It's no wonder the devil desperately tries to keep us far away from God's Word!

THE POWER OF
THE PRESENT TENSE

I sure am glad 1 John 3:1 was written for us in the present tense (NIV): "See what great love the Father has lavished on us, that we should be called children of God! And that is what we are!" Just imagine if this scripture had been penned in the *past* tense, something like, "What great love the father *had* lavished on us, that we *used to be* called children of God. And that is what you *were* before you went and screwed everything up, you big dummy!" Thank God it doesn't say that! But why do I spend so much of my life defeated by the thought that somehow my days as a chosen child of God have run out, or that his promises have expired? When I start to feel spiritually defeated like that, my Bible is the last thing I feel like reading. That's all part of the evil one's plan. Satan hates it when we read God's Word.

Haven't you ever wondered why it is so difficult to maintain a daily quiet time, but it's so easy to flip the television on and waste away the hours watching some mindless reality television show? In my personal spiritual journey, I wrestle daily with committing to read my Bible. A couple years ago, I signed up for one of those online plans with the goal of reading through the entire Bible in a year. Confession: It took me a year and a half. And I know the reason why. Satan throws any distraction or addition to my to-do list that he can think of, stealing my attention away from God's promises and sending me on some needless detour. As I have grown in my faith over the years, I have also grown in disciplining myself to guard my daily time with God and to tell the enemy to back off when he approaches. But this is still a struggle.

Now, on the days we *do* read our Bible and successfully deflect the devil's attempts to keep us away from God's Word, what do you think happens? Do you think Satan stops there, throws up a white flag, and says, "Oh well, lost one to the good guys"? No, the battle heats up even more. I'm sure you've witnessed this heightened attack in your own life. And here is one way I've seen Satan at work even when I get past his first hurdles: he is the master of twisted Scripture. I know God's Word. I've been memorizing Scripture since my childhood days at Vacation Bible School. Back then the prize for whoever memorized the most Bible verses was a giant, three-foot-long candy bar (which was really several Butterfinger candy bars taped to a measuring stick). As a kid, that was all the motivation I needed. These days I'm just as motivated to know God's Word so that Satan no longer poses a threat to my identity. The more I know about what God's Word says, the easier it is to remind myself who God says I am when I'm under attack. Satan might say, "Yeah, you *were* a child of God, but that was long ago. You've made too many mistakes, you're disqualified." But because I have God's Word hidden in my heart, I know that in this very moment, even when I feel far away from him, I am deeply loved by him and I am his beloved child. I know who my best friend is and I know what my best friend thinks of me. I know what he says about me. Nothing Satan throws at me can take the truth I know away.

Hebrews describes the Word of God as "alive and powerful. It is sharper than the sharpest two-edged sword" (4:12 NIV). A sword in the wrong hands can be a weapon used to injure, damage, wound, kill. But a sword in the right hands can be like a scalpel in the hands of a surgeon—a tool of precision intended to fix, to heal. This is the difference between God's plans for you and Satan's intentions. The deceiver will twist the very Scripture written to give us life, turning present tense "I am a child of God" into "I was a child of God." He will attempt to make this two-edged sword his weapon, cutting us down by convincing us that we could never live up to God's standards.

There are nights right before I walk on stage to sing for people when I hear the voice of the father of lies shout something in my heart like, *Who do you think you are going out there to sing about God's grace? You've abused God's grace so many times. What a hypocrite!* His timing is impeccable. He knows that from the stage I am going to have a great opportunity to share my testimony and remind thousands of people who they are in Christ. It makes me think of the final scene in the movie *Gladiator*, where the movie's hero, Maximus, enters the Colosseum for a final face-off with the evil emperor. But the emperor does not play fair. He discreetly stabs Maximus upon their greeting, leaving him wounded and gasping for breath before their battle even begins, weakening the mighty warrior. That's how Satan works on a spiritual level. Sometimes he attacks when you're weakest. Other times he will attack when you're right on the verge of greatness. Either way he, like the emperor, doesn't play by the rules.

These preshow battles have become a regular occurrence for me. As a means of spiritual survival, I have begun to develop a routine in anticipation of the enemy's whispers. Just before walking on stage, I open the Bible app on my phone and read Scripture until I hear my name announced and the music begins. Nothin' like the truth to block out the noise of a lie and keep the devil at bay. After all, that's how Jesus himself handled Satan's attacks.

When Jesus was led into the wilderness where he fasted for forty days and nights, I cannot even imagine how he felt. Now, when I've fasted before for a day or two, or maybe a week, I couldn't even get a few hours in before I started seeing mirages of ice cream cones and BBQ spare ribs. I remember feeling so weak. Satan must have thought Jesus would be weak from his fast, so when Jesus was alone, that's when he attacked Jesus's identity and tempted him to sin by twisting Scripture. If Satan is willing to go after the identity of the very Son of God, you better believe he's going to come after you and me. And guess what Jesus used to fend off Satan's temptation? God's Word. With every temptation thrown at him by the father of lies, Jesus's response began with this three word declaration: "It is written." And each time Jesus responded with the truth of Scripture, Satan was put back on his heels until he finally gave up. "Then the devil went away" (Matthew 4:11).

Imagine having the power to make the devil give up trying to steal your identity just like Jesus did. Okay, now stop imagining it and take hold of the promise that you, too, have been given this same power through Scripture: "I have hidden your word in my heart, that I might not sin against you" (Psalm 119:11). Hiding God's Word in your heart is ultimately what will make Satan run and hide. "Resist the devil, and he will flee from you" (James 4:7). Notice the power of the present tense on display with these identity-affirming verses throughout Scripture:

> Therefore, if anyone is in Christ, He is a new creation. (2 Corinthians 5:17 ESV)

> Therefore, there is now no condemnation for those who are in Christ Jesus. (Romans 8:1 NIV)

My grace is sufficient for you, for my power is made perfect in weakness. (2 Corinthians 12:8)

For by grace you have been saved through faith . . . it is the gift of God. (Ephesians 2:8 ESV)

The next time you feel like your identity is under attack by the enemy, remember that you can combat Satan's *past-tense* lies with God's *present-tense* truths and respond with confidence, "It is written, I am a new creation. It is written, there is now no condemnation. It is written, God's grace is sufficient for me. It is written, I am saved by grace. It is written, I have been called a child of God, and that is what I am!"

ALL THINGS FOR THE GOOD?

If there was a top ten list for most popular Bible verses, I have to believe Romans 8:28 would be somewhere near the top. "And we know that in all things God works for the good of those who love him, who have been called according to his purpose" (NIV). What's not to love about that? It's sort of a spiritual safety net, isn't it? What an empowering promise that anything in our lives can be something God uses for good! But our scouting report on our enemy is trying to warn us that though God works all things for the good, Satan intends to use all things for evil in your life. The word *perversion* in Hebrew means "bent" or "twisted." We've already seen how Satan twists Scripture, but he won't stop there. Everything that happens in our lives can be the birth of something positive or something perverse, depending on which voice we choose to listen to.

- **Success?** God wants your success in life to create in you a thankful heart. Satan wants success to make you prideful, greedy, and constantly unfulfilled.
- **Trials?** Our Father can use trials to make us God-dependent. Satan will use them to stir up the feeling that we need to take control and become self-sufficient.
- **Tragedy?** We can emerge from our deepest heart-breaks better, stronger, and longing for heaven. Or we can turn bitter, weaker, and lose sight of eternity.
- **Sin?** God wants you to be grace-filled. Satan wants to leave you guilt-ridden.
- **Love?** God can show you the meaning of true love. Satan wants you to settle for lust.

Satan has a scouting report of his own. He's aware of our strengths and weaknesses, our blessings and our trials. He knows what we are capable of in our finest hour and our weakest moment. He watches every move and waits for the opportune time, "looking for someone to devour" (1 Peter 5:8). So we can't afford to live in denial about the areas of life where we know we might be susceptible to temptation or moral failure.

This whole book is really about honesty. And being honest

about ourselves is not only important when thinking of the potential for greatness we have as God's chosen children, but also when thinking of the potential for epic failure. We are only a choice or two away from one or the other. John Ortberg talks about the importance of knowing not just our mission in life, but our shadow mission as well. As you might imagine, your shadow mission is opposite of your God-planned mission in life. Ortberg wrote in *Overcoming Your Shadow Mission*, "If we fail to embrace our true mission, we will live out our shadow mission. We will let our lives center around things that are unworthy, selfish, and dark."

God knows what your shadow mission is. The enemy knows what your shadow mission is. Do you know what your shadow mission is? It's really difficult to take that honest look in the mirror and ask yourself, *What am I capable of if I don't keep God at the center of my life?* Have you ever observed a poor life choice someone has made, maybe a friend's moral failure, and thought to yourself, *I can't believe they did that*, or *That would never happen to me*. Chances are, that person once thought the same thing.

Are you living your shadow mission right now and wondering how you wound up so far from where God was calling you? He is still calling you. Calling you out of the darkness of your shadow mission and into his "marvelous light" (1 Peter 2:9 ESV). Once again, God never said that all things *are* good. He said he works all things *for* good. For the good of those who are "called according to his purpose." The thief may have stolen your identity. You may not even know who you are anymore. But God still knows you. God still calls you, and God still has a purpose for you, a mission only you can accomplish.

Considering the names given to Satan in Scripture, what destructive intentions does he have for your life, and how does he try to steal your spiritual identity?

What mission are you embracing right now—the one God is calling you to, or your shadow mission keeping you from his "marvelous light"?

Read 1 John 3:1. How does the present tense of this verse make a difference in your life? If it were written in past tense, how would that change things?

CHAPTER 10

GRACE WINS
EVERY TIME

Here come those whispers in my ear saying,
"Who do you think you are?
Looks like you're on your own from here.
Grace could never reach that far."

"GRACE WINS"

Everyone feared Rob would die young. Including Rob. Even his drug dealer told him he should slow down. Drug of choice? Heroin, which goes from being a drug of choice to a drug of necessity in no time. But Rob was convinced it was everyone else who had a problem, not him. And he wouldn't let anyone stop him from living his life the way he wanted to. Not a brand-new baby. Not the pleading cries of his parents. In and out of trouble. In and out of jail. Rob's story was headed for a heartbreaking ending, and those who loved him were forced to stand by helplessly, watching him destroy the best years of his young life.

The summer of 2014 found Rob in a familiar place, behind bars. His mother agreed to bail him out once more, but this time on one condition: that he go with her to a Christian music concert at the Kentucky State Fair. Rob reluctantly agreed, and a couple of days later a mother and her drug-addicted son sat in the grandstand waiting for my concert to begin. Before the show, my band and I gathered backstage and prayed for what was about to happen. We pray a similar prayer every night:

Lord, we pray for tonight to be more than just a show. We pray for your presence to be so real that no one in the crowd can deny it. We pray for hearts to turn to you, for chains to be broken, and for lives to be changed. We don't know every person in the audience, but you do. We ask you to speak through us in a powerful way. Amen.

Little did I know that Rob was in the audience and that I wasn't the only one praying for him. His mother had desperately been praying for her son to hear from God that night. During the concert, I performed the song that inspired the theme of this book, *Hello, My Name Is*. But before singing, I played a video on the screen behind me that told the story of Jordan (whom you read about at the beginning of this book) and his own battle with drug addiction. In his own words, Jordan told the crowd about going from all-American athlete to college dropout, and how difficult it had been living with the shame, guilt, and regret over the mistakes he had made and the people he had hurt. He shared through tears how God stepped in and changed his life.

His story was like an arrow aimed straight at the heart of Rob, another young man who had lost all hope that God could still love him. Rob told me later that he saw himself on that video screen that night, and as Jordan told his story, he thought, *If God can change Jordan, maybe he can change me too.* Moments later, I gave an invitation for anyone in the crowd that night who needed to lay down some old nametags and false identities to take the bold step of raising their hand and surrendering their life to Jesus. Rob prayed, and his mom rejoiced.

But that defining moment at the concert was only the first step of Rob's remarkable turnaround. He went home from the concert and e-mailed the ministry that I started with my dad called pop**we**, whose mission is to go beyond just musical entertainment and to let hurting people know their stories matter and their stories are far from over. The ministry offers prayer, support, and connection to other helpful resources during a time of crisis and walks with people on their road to discovering the greater story God has for each of us.

Rob told us that he wanted to get help for his addiction but didn't know where to start and couldn't afford the cost. My dad told Rob that if he was willing to go, our ministry would make sure there were no obstacles in his way. After a few weeks of Rob wrestling with his demons, agreeing to go and then changing his mind, he told my dad he was finally ready. We were able to get him into the exact same Teen Challenge treatment facility from which Jordan graduated. Pretty amazing how God works, isn't it?

Rob has now been clean and sober for two years. The transformation in his life is undeniable and has even led to him being offered a job with that same drug-recovery program. One of the most incredible full-circle moments I have ever witnessed was seeing him return to one of my concerts a year later in Norfolk, Virginia. The circumstances of his attendance at this show were much different from the first time he attended simply to appease his mom. This time Rob was clean, sober, his eyes were clear, and there was a smile on his face. What's more, he hadn't come alone. He brought with him a group of young men who had just entered into recovery and he was now mentoring. That night I sang the song I wrote for him titled "Grace Wins." These words were inspired by his remarkable transformation.

No more lying down in death's defeat,
I'm rising up in victory
Singing hallelujah grace wins every time!

At the end of the song, Rob walked onstage to a standing ovation from fifteen thousand people. As applause filled the arena, I thought about those young men being mentored by Rob. They were teenagers who were struggling. Struggling to see past the guilt of their own addictions. Struggling to believe that something good could still come of their lives. Struggling to believe that God still loved them despite the mess they had landed in. But there they were, watching Rob and listening to an entire arena cheering him on, a guy who just a year before was down and out like they were. I smiled to think that maybe God was aiming his arrows of grace straight at the hearts of those young men the way he did to Rob on the night he took his first step toward freedom.

GUILT VS. GRACE

Satan tried everything he could to keep Rob off of the path to freedom. He does the same to you and me. While we would tend to think that sin is what keeps us from embracing our identity in Christ, *guilt* actually is the enemy's craftiest of tricks. If sin is what knocks us down, guilt is what *keeps* us down. Sin and guilt are Satan's one-two punch, and with guilt he keeps kicking us while we're down, reminding us how we messed up and telling us that we are beyond the point of no return. Guilt is what kept Rob from coming to God for so long.

The Bible talks about a spiritual warfare that is waged for our souls. A war between guilt and grace, good and evil, God's truth and Satan's lies. "This is for keeps, a life-or-death fight to the finish against the Devil and all his angels" (Ephesians 6:12 MSG). Guilt and grace share only one thing: they both want our attention. Beyond that, they stand in stark contrast to one another, as opposite as Scripture says—choosing between the two is a matter of *life or death* to our spiritual lives.

Guilt says, "You're broken beyond repair."
Grace says, "Get ready to be healed beyond belief" (Psalm 30:2).

Guilt says, "You're too far gone."
Grace says, "You're just one step away from home" (John 3:16).

Guilt says, "You're nothing but damaged goods."
Grace says, "You're something good in the making" (Philippians 1:6).

Guilt says, "Your best days are behind you."
Grace says, "The best is yet to come" (1 Corinthians 2:9).

Guilt says, "You're wounded."
Grace says, "I was wounded so you could be mended" (Isaiah 53:5).

Guilt says, "You'll never escape your past."
Grace says, "Your sins are remembered no more" (Isaiah 43:25).

Guilt says, "You're helpless."
Grace says, "I will help you if you just ask" (Hebrews 13:6).

Guilt says, "How could you?"
Grace says, "How could you ever doubt my love?" (Matthew 14:31).

Rob felt the push and pull of those competing voices. I've heard them. And I'm sure you've heard them too. Satan wants us to believe in his guilt-lies over God's grace-truth, because then we'll believe that our sins and mistakes disqualify us from receiving anything good from our Father in heaven. Satan knows that if he can lower our eyes, we'll remain focused on what we've done instead of what God has done for us. Guilt pushed Adam and Eve away from God in the garden of Eden. Guilt pushed Judas, a flawed disciple, to the point of suicide crushed by the weight of his betrayal of Jesus. Guilt pushed Peter back out on to a boat to resume his old life as a fisherman, figuring, *I've denied Christ three times, my best days are behind me.* When all we see is what we've done, things sure start to look hopeless in a hurry.

But while guilt pushes, grace reaches. With the arms of a loving father, grace reached for a prodigal son coming home. Through a lone voice in a crowd of accusers, grace reached for a woman caught in the act of adultery. From the Savior on the center cross, grace assured a thief dying next to him, "Today you will be with me in paradise" (Luke 23:43 NIV). Grace reached for Rob. Grace reached for me. And grace has reached for you. "But God demonstrates his own love for us in this: while we were still sinners, Christ died for us" (Romans 5:8). The arms of grace reached from heaven all the way to earth, and God's only Son defeated the power of sin and guilt once and for all.

Grace invites us to stop looking at our sin and start "fixing our eyes on Jesus . . . [who] endured the cross" (Hebrews 12:2).

Grace reaches out to your nametag and begins crossing out the lies one by one, saying, "You are not your shame. You are not your sin. You are not your guilt." There is "no condemnation for those who belong to Christ Jesus. And because you belong to him, the power of the life-giving Spirit has freed you from the power of sin that leads to death" (Romans 8:1–2).

I GOT SAVED A LOT

I was convinced on more than one occasion growing up that the rapture had taken place and I had been left behind. My family and I lived in a little blue house behind the church where my dad was the pastor. The only thing that separated the church from my backyard was a field where we used to host picnics after summer services. My brothers and I created a well-worn path back and forth from our house to Dad's office at the church. One Sunday night our church watched the 1970s faith-based movie *A Thief in the Night*, and it really messed me up.

The movie depicts the aftermath of the second coming of Christ. Certain images are forever burned in my memory. One minute, this guy is mowing his lawn. The next, the lawn mower is left running, but the guy is gone. A woman puts butter in a frying pan while preparing breakfast in her kitchen, and in the next scene the frying pan is unattended and the smoke detector is going off. There were people screaming and weeping when they woke up to a half-empty bed. Car wrecks on the highway. One chilling scene after the other showed me what it would be like if I wasn't ready when Jesus came back. Perhaps you've seen the more recent version of this movie called *Left Behind*. Well,

I haven't seen it. I won't either. The first version scared me to death! Actually, to be more accurate, it scared me to life. What I mean is, I must have seen that film about ten times, and after each viewing, I asked Jesus into my heart all over again, just in case it didn't stick the first nine times.

Growing up, it was not uncommon for me and my brothers to return home from school only to find that my parents were hard at work at the church across the field. Before I watched this movie I never even thought twice about where Mom and Dad might be. But after being terrified by the unmanned lawn-mower? I was on high alert. I remember hopping off the school bus and skipping toward home. I noticed the front door was left open. I called out, "Mom? Dad?" I noticed their car was in the driveway. "Mom! Dad!" I yelled louder. No answer. My heart started pounding. My feet hit that well-worn path on the field between my house and our church, and I had never run so fast in my life. I bet if I had been timed during those runs, I could have qualified for the Olympics. Throwing open the church doors I yelled again, "Dad! Mom! Are you here?" "Yes, son, what's wrong?" my mom responded calmly, wondering why I was out of breath. "Oh, uh . . . ," I mumbled while trying to gain my composure. "Nothing. I was, uh, just wondering, uh, where you were."

I'd like to tell you that only happened once, but I'd be lying. After every scare, I remember going into the sanctuary of the church, hitting my knees, and praying, "God, forgive me . . . again! I want to be ready! I don't want to be left behind!"

When was the last time you had a clear conscience? A clear

conscience is proof that we have fully taken hold of the freedom we have been given in Christ. I look back now and laugh at those moments of fear and uncertainty, guilt and panic. I was a kid with a cloudy conscience. Those were the actions of someone who hadn't fully embraced the freedom grace offers. As I have been under spiritual construction in the years since those childhood days, I am learning that being a work in progress doesn't mean I'm not a new creation. I cannot live afraid that with every wrong turn I've lost what I once had found. "From eternity to eternity I am God. No one can snatch anyone out of my hand. No one can undo what I have done" (Isaiah 43:13). A new creation is free to move forward with a clear conscience. That sounds good, doesn't it? "Sin is no longer your master, for you no longer live under the requirements of the law. Instead, you live under the freedom of God's grace" (Romans 6:14). Grace has torn in a million little pieces the list of sins that Satan has held in front of you for so long. Imagine the list of every sin you've ever committed, every mistake you've ever made in your entire life being torn and tossed into the air like confetti at a New Year's Day parade. Because for a new creation, every day is New Year's Day. And when you live like that, you get excited for what God is going to do in your life next.

DREAM AGAIN

God has done a pretty cool work through stories of recovery like Jordan's and Rob's and the songs they inspired. I now get the opportunity to invite men and women from local recovery groups like Teen Challenge or Celebrate Recovery to my concerts as my guests. I do this in the hopes that just like Rob, they will hear from God in a powerful way and be reminded who he says they are. One night before the concert, I stood in front of a group of about twenty men who had accepted my invitation to attend the show. I could see by the looks on their faces that many of them were attending their first Christian music concert. It was evident that these guys were all in different stages of their recovery journey. I had been told that a few of the men had only arrived to the treatment facility days before. I spoke up, thanking the guys for coming to the show, and went on to tell them what my hope for them was. But I was interrupted in the best way. As I was telling the guys, "My prayer for you tonight is that you will be inspired to—" a voice from the group spoke up and finished my sentence with two words, "dream again."

Somewhat stunned, my eyes found the eyes of the guy I was sure spoke those words. I could see it. He wanted so badly for someone to give him permission to stop beating himself up about his past. He wanted so badly to see the chains of his addiction break once and for all. He wanted to feel alive again. He wanted to be free again. He wanted to dream again. "Yes," I said. "That's it! Dream again. I pray you guys leave this concert inspired to dream again and know that God has a huge dream for your lives!" With that, we huddled together, a group of broken men calling on the name of a healing God, asking him to rid us of our burdensome past once and for all and to give us permission to dream a new dream.

That's my prayer for you, even right now. A prayer for you to dream a new dream. The moment you confess your sins and run into the open arms of grace that have reached for you, your name becomes "New Creation." And as a new creation, you are free to start dreaming a new dream. You are not a finished product. God is refining you day by day, renewing you moment by moment. You are loved, you are forgiven, you are a new creation, and you are free to dream a new dream.

In what areas of your life are grace and guilt battling it out? Which one is winning right now?

Can you be a "new creation" while still a "work in progress"? How does Satan want you to answer that? What does Jesus want you to believe?

Read Isaiah 43:13 and Romans 6:14. How do these verses help you break free from Satan's lies so you can once again believe in Jesus's grace and start to dream again?

THE
FUTURE
YOU

Living Your Life as
a Child of the One True King

CHAPTER 11

PICK A NAME, ANY NAME

Don't be afraid, I've redeemed you.
I've called your name. You're mine.

ISAIAH 43:1 MSG

O f the many difficult decisions a parent must make, I have encountered none more challenging than one that comes even before a baby is born: *picking a name!* This process was pure agony for my wife and me. I am so glad that we were not around when God was looking to place someone in charge of naming all of the animals in the garden of Eden. If it had been left up to us, some of God's creatures would still be roaming the earth without a name. The task of naming our youngest daughter was especially difficult. Come to think of it, I bet that's why God designed a nine-month pregnancy. Not so that we could get the baby's room ready. But because he knew we humans would likely need three full trimesters just to agree on a name. God really does think of everything.

As we turned the corner toward the final weeks of my wife's pregnancy, we began to grow nervous since neither one of us had a strong sense of what we should name our little girl. So I made a plan. I booked a reservation at our favorite restaurant, and we agreed that neither of us would leave that dinner table until nailing down the perfect name. Three hours later, we had a long list of contenders, but still no unanimous decision. Frustrated with each other, we finally left the restaurant as they closed down for the night, but we vowed to try again the next day. Still nothing!

A few short weeks later, my wife went into labor, and before we knew it an amazing, incredible, healthy, beautiful, little girl was placed in our arms as we cried, hugged, took pictures, and counted fingers and toes. The doctor said, "Congratulations! What's her name?" That's when it hit us. In all of the chaos and excitement of the delivery, we forgot that we had yet to land on a name! Embarrassed and with the pressure mounting, we told the doctor that we were still deciding. So our little girl entered into the world on day one officially nameless.

Forty-eight hours later, a sassy, southern nurse brought our newborn daughter into our hospital room and hit us with an ultimatum. "You know we can't let you leave this hospital until you pick a name for your little girl. Just pick one and go with it!" She made it sound so easy. But then she said something that really hit me. "Besides," she said, "we nurses like to call every baby by his or her name when we are caring for them in the nursery, and we've just been referring to yours as 'Baby West.'"

Well, that was it. I refused to let her be called "Baby West" a second longer. We pulled out our list from the restaurant. We prayed together. And right there in the hospital room, we miraculously landed on her name: Delaney Ruth West. I wrote the song "Safe and Sound" when our first child was born, and now the lyrics conveyed exactly what I was feeling the moments after we decided what name Delaney would carry with her for the rest of her life:

> We couldn't wait to meet you,
> hope you like your name . . .

Seven years later, it seems my daughter's name suits her just fine. I kept the original list of names from that night at the restaurant as a reminder that while her mom and I were indecisively going back and forth, and while the nurses were calling her "Baby West," she was already known. "Before I shaped you in the womb, I knew all about you" (Jeremiah 1:5 MSG). Her Creator knew every single detail of her life before she breathed her first breath. "You saw me before I was born. Every day of my life was recorded in your book. Every moment was laid out before a single day had passed" (Psalm 139:16). The same goes for you. You were God's idea. He saw you as someone worth creating. Someone worth loving. He knows you on a deeper level than anyone else ever has or ever will.

ON A NICKNAME BASIS

"Buddy." "Pal." "Honey." "Sweetie." "Dude." Ever been called by one of these nicknames? These kinds of names are a generic acknowledgment we might use when we don't really remember the name of the person we are talking to. The music industry is famous for this kind of talk. Mostly because people are always looking over your shoulder in case someone they deem more important than you shows up. For years, there was one person I always seemed to run into at industry events, and he would greet me by saying, "Hey, man!" But he would drag out the end of the word, "Hey, m*aaaaaa*," keeping the *n* silent. I always interpreted this to mean that he was about 50 percent sure my name was "Matt," but just in case he was wrong, it would sound like he was just calling me "man." Very clever. But I saw right through it, and I always wanted to respond with, "Good to see you, too, *buddy*."

There are different kinds of nicknames that are more endearing than a "Hey, man." These are the kind developed as almost a second language among the closest of friends or family. My band members are prime examples of this. We spend half of our lives in close quarters on a tour bus, and with all of the different experiences and laughs we share together, we have created some pretty funny nicknames for each other that wouldn't make sense to anyone outside of our tight-knit crew. Our bass player's name is Dave, but we call him "Chili." There's Jake on lead guitar, but we call him "Jake from State Farm." We've got Sean on the drums, but we call him "Chorizo."

It seems the more comfortable we become in a relationship, the more likely we are to develop special nicknames for each other. This is even true for our daughter Delaney. On any given day I'll find myself referring to her as "Lane," "Laney," "Ladybug," "Bug," "Wayne-y," "John Wayne," "Olivia Newton John-Wayne." (I couldn't even tell you how I got to those last two!) But for us, it's less about what the actual nicknames are and more about what they represent—the closeness we share with each other, small symbols of affection.

God has nicknames for us too. Each one gives us more insight into how deep his love is for us and how much we matter to him. These are just a few of my favorite nicknames given to us by our Creator in Scripture.

He calls us *beloved.* "My beloved is mine and I am his" (Song of Songs 2:16 NIV).

He calls us *friends.* "I have called you friends" (John 15:15 NIV).

He calls us his *treasured possession.* "The LORD your God has chosen you out of all the peoples on the face of the earth to be his people, his treasured possession" (Deuteronomy 7:6 NIV).

He calls us the *apple of his eye.* "Keep me as the apple of your eye; hide me in the shadow of your wings" (Psalm 17:8 NIV).

He calls us *blessed.* "Blessed is the one you choose and bring near, to dwell in your courts" (Psalm 65:4 ESV).

He calls us *redeemed*. "In him we have redemption through his blood" (Ephesians 1:7 NIV).

He calls us *sons and daughters*. "I will be a Father to you, and you will be my sons and daughters, says the Lord Almighty" (2 Corinthians 6:18 NIV).

Just as with the list of baby names from the restaurant I keep as a reminder of the time we were deciding on Delaney's name, this is a list worth keeping nearby when we need to remind ourselves of our true worth. These nicknames God has for us not only describe how much he loves us, but how much he knows us and how close he wants us to be to him. The world sure has a way of making us doubt our value or significance, but God isn't about to let you forget who he says you are.

HELLO, MY NAME IS "UNWANTED"

One of the most defeating experiences in anyone's life is when your name simply isn't called at all. Can you think of a moment when you would have given anything to have your name called but it wasn't? Maybe you can recall moments like these:

The results of the high school musical auditions were posted on the choir room door Monday morning, and everyone, including you, raced to see who got what part. Your name was nowhere to be found. *Untalented.*

You really felt a special connection after a couple of dates, but she has stopped calling. You keep checking your phone, but no missed calls or texts to be found. *Unloved.*

You thought you had a best friend until that friend threw a party and you weren't invited, and you found out about it through social media posts. *Uninvited.*

Your birth parents decided they could not raise you, and you've yet to find a forever family, still bouncing around from foster home to foster home. *Unwanted.*

I recently returned home from performing a concert in a small town outside of Charlotte, North Carolina, where I was invited to be part of a fund-raiser for an organization called Least of These, started by two moms who have made it their mission to pour into the lives of foster children. Susanna and Michelle are fearless fighters for these kids, and spending just five minutes with them hearing their hearts, I was convinced that God had brought me there for a reason.

"It's all your fault, you know," Susanna said to me with a smirk as we sat in what appeared to be the pastor's office in the church where the concert was held. "Why's that?" I asked. "You had to go and write that song 'Do Something.' That's what got me into this whole thing," she said with a sarcastically accusatory tone. This wasn't the first time that song or I had been jokingly blamed for someone stepping out in faith and daring to be about a greater cause. The lyrics of that song are a challenge not to wait around for someone else to do something about the injustices we see around us but to recognize that maybe God has in mind for us to be that someone. The lyrics say, "If not us then who? If not me and you, right now. It's time for us to do something." Suzanne shared how the message of that song had resonated with her deeply and how she had been unable to escape the feeling that God was stirring up a desire in her heart to do something about these kids who desperately needed to know they are valued and loved.

Susanna and Michelle then told me a little bit about some of the children I would soon be meeting and singing for. I learned that the children who are placed in these group homes don't get to have their birthdays celebrated individually. Instead, they do a group celebration for the kids all having birthdays within a three-month period. Can you imagine your actual birthday coming and going without even a mention from those closest to you? Perhaps you know that feeling. No one should ever experience that. Susanna told me they host a summer camp for all of the kids in foster care each year. She said that on more than one occasion a child has approached her and quietly asked, "Why doesn't anyone want me?" I found it hard to breathe for a few seconds while I lingered under the weight of that question, and it wasn't even a question directed at me. Then they told me they have heard this question more times than their hearts can handle since starting this ministry. *Why doesn't anyone want me?* Such heartbreaking words from heartbroken children who can't understand why they weren't seen as a kid worth keeping, a name worth knowing, a life worth loving.

YOU ARE KNOWN

Zacchaeus was a guy who had been overlooked his entire life. Literally. He was short in stature, even shorter on character. As the chief tax collector, he had gained a reputation as one of the most hated men in Jericho because he was a thief and a cheat. One day crowds gathered in his town as Jesus came through, but since Zacchaeus couldn't see, he climbed high up into a tree to get a better view. What happened next shocked everyone, including Zacchaeus. When Jesus came by, he looked up at him and called him by name. "Zacchaeus!" he said. "Quick, come down! I must be a guest in your home today" (Luke 19:5). His name had been called. Jesus knew who he was. *But how?* he must have thought. *Why me?* he must have wondered. But there was no time for questions. No time for self-doubt. Instead, "Zacchaeus quickly climbed down and took Jesus to his house in great excitement and joy" (v. 6).

Scripture points out that the people who saw this exchange were displeased that Jesus picked Zacchaeus. But notice how their opinions didn't matter to him anymore. He hopped down from that tree and hung out with Jesus in "great excitement and joy." This is what hearing your name called by the Savior will do. It will drown out the opinions of a thousand other voices. He was no longer unwanted, no longer felt unloved. Jesus saw him. Jesus knew him. Jesus called him by name.

Jesus chose Zacchaeus that day, and this is what Jesus still does today. It does not matter how others have failed you, forgotten you, labeled you, or overlooked you. He sees you. He knows you. He calls you by name. You are wanted. And he has chosen you.

My dad is notoriously good at remembering peoples' names. As he's gotten older, he has only become more diligent in his efforts to recall someone's name, even if it's been a long time between encounters. In order to do this, he has taken up writing notes. He keeps a little note pad with him, and in it he writes the names of people he meets so he can refer to them later and commit them to memory. Your heavenly Father has written your name down, and he has never forgotten your name. And he never will.

> Can a mother forget the infant at her breast,
>   walk away from the baby she bore?
> But even if mothers forget,
>   I'd never forget you—never.
> Look, I've written your names on the backs of my
>   hands. (Isaiah 49:15–16 MSG)

God says, "Look," as if he is holding out his hands to show us what he means. Our names written on the palms of his hands. But when I close my eyes and try to picture this image, I don't see my name. I see scars. Scars from the nails that held him to a cross. Scars that say, "You are not forgotten. You are irreplaceable. Look at my scars and know this is how much you matter. This is how much you are wanted. This is how well you are known. This is how deeply you are loved."

Look up the meaning of your name. How does it fit who you are? Can you think of any name(s) you wish your parents had given you instead?

Look over the list of "nicknames" that God gives us. How do they give you insight into God's deep love for you and how much you matter to him?

Read the story of Zacchaeus in Luke 19. How do you think he felt when Jesus noticed him? How does it make you feel to know that God has never forgotten your name and never will?

CHAPTER 12

NAME CHANGER, GAME CHANGER

God loves you just the way you are,
but he refuses to leave you that way.
MAX LUCADO

I love football. And I love the nicknames some NFL players earn because of their playing style. Deion Sanders was known as "Prime Time" because of his knack for showing up big in the big games. Marshawn Lynch was referred to as "Beast Mode" because of that powerful extra gear he seemed to possess, making him impossible for defenders to bring down as he ran over them and broke tackles. Linebacker Jack Tatum was known as "The Assassin" because he was the hardest-hitting free safety of his time. One of my childhood heroes, the late, great Walter Payton, was referred to by Chicago Bears fans as "Sweetness" thanks to his fancy footwork that helped him dance into the end zone over and over again. And "Mean" Joe Greene, well, he was just plain mean.

I dreamed of one day picking up a name like that. Trying out for the high school football team was never even a question. In high school I cared about one thing. Okay, maybe two things: girls and sports. But not in that order. Sports came first, hands down. Baseball, basketball, football. The big three. I loved 'em all, and I played 'em all year round. I wasn't really built to be a football player—not especially tall or big or strong or fast—but that did not stop me. My freshman year I set a goal that by the time I was a senior, I wouldn't just be a starter on the varsity team, but I would be the team captain. I'd be known for my fierce determination and no-quit attitude. I would be a leader of men, a god of the gridiron. I imagined earning nicknames such as Matthew "The Monster" West or "Mad Dog" Matthew. You know, something cool like that with a strong use of alliteration.

This is the story of how one of the most exciting moments of my life became one of the most embarrassing moments of my life . . .

At the end of every football season, a chosen few under-classmen would be called up to the varsity team on its journey through the playoffs. The coaches did this to give some of the young guys a little experience to prepare them for their next year on the varsity team. This was my mission, to perform well enough during my sophomore season that I would be selected, and it happened. I was so excited. My friend Jeff and I got to dress with the big boys and travel with the team to the play-offs! Of course, my buddy and I knew that we had no chance of seeing any real game action, but it didn't matter. We were just happy to be there. We were in varsity uniforms, riding the varsity bus, part of the varsity team! We were pumped just to be standing on the sidelines soaking up the entire experience.

Well, the team was looking good. We made it through a couple rounds of the playoffs, and as we went further into the postseason, the weather was getting colder by the week. The next round of the playoffs led us to East St. Louis on a bitterly cold day. I mean, the kind of cold where you see your breath and you can't feel your toes. Jeff and I, knowing we were about to spend several hours standing on the sidelines, thought it would be smart to dress for an arctic excursion. So we piled on the layers. I wore two pairs of long underwear, two pairs of socks, plus a turtleneck and hoodie under my shoulder pads and jersey. Looking like Ralphie, the little brother from *A Christmas Story*, when he got dressed to walk to school ("I can't put my arms down!"), I could barely move. If I fell over, I wasn't standing back up without assistance. But it didn't matter, because a sophomore on the varsity sidelines wasn't going to be doing much moving unless I had to go to the bathroom.

The Trojans were on fire that day. By the fourth quarter we were ahead by a score of 35–0. That's when the unthinkable happened. "West, you're in!" the coach shouted in my direction. I was sure my ears were suffering from frostbite and I must have misheard him. He shouted again, "West, hustle! Get in there!" My fellow sophomore teammate looked at me with a big grin and said with a shove, "This is your chance!" I took off running onto the field as fast as I could and joined the huddle with the rest of the defense. I was sent in to play right defensive end, and East St. Louis was closing in on their first touchdown of the game with the ball on the five-yard line. The play was called and I ran up to the line to get in my stance. My heart was pounding. Was this really happening? There was no way this team was going to score a touchdown on my watch. This was the beginning of my "Mad Dog" legacy.

But just as the other team approached the line across from me, I looked down and noticed something very wrong. For the entire game, I had been wearing a pair of giant baby-blue mittens in order to keep my hands warm on the sidelines. In all of the excitement, I had forgotten to take them off, and now it was too late. The ball was snapped. The quarterback tossed the ball to the running back. *Please don't run toward me. Please don't run toward me,* I thought. And as though he read my mind . . . he began running in my direction. The game slipped into slow motion at that point. I shed one blocker and got in position to tackle the running back, and all of a sudden I was the only thing between that runner and the goal line. I dove in his direction and wrapped my arms around his legs for the tackle. But the mittens wouldn't let me get a firm enough grip to pull him to the ground. He slipped right through and high-stepped his way into the end zone, spiking the ball and celebrating with his teammates. So long, "Mad Dog." Hello, my name is Matthew "Mittens" West. Hey, at least there's alliteration.

It took even longer to shed that unwanted name than it did to shed the many layers of long underwear following my humiliating playoff debut. Only after achieving my goal of being voted team captain by coaches and teammates my senior season did the name "Mittens" finally get laid to rest. It was that one embarrassing first playoff moment that motivated me along the way. I was determined to be known for something more than my mitten mistake, and it felt so gratifying the day the coach announced to the team that I was the captain. Captain Mittens, I guess.

JACOB AND THE SEVEN DWARFS

No one wants to be known for flaws, mistakes, or blunders. The things we like least about ourselves are the things we try hardest to keep out of the spotlight. After spending a season being known as "Mittens," it makes me wonder how some of Snow White's Seven Dwarfs must have felt. I wonder if Dopey, Grumpy, Sleepy, and Bashful were ever like, "Hey, Snow White, if it's cool with you, can we revisit the whole name thing?" While accurate descriptors of some of their personality traits, those names are anything but flattering. But cartoon characters aren't the only ones with reason to resent their given names.

In ancient times, birth names were sometimes given as an indication of a certain facet of someone's character or disposition. There is a Hebrew folk saying implying that a person's name could be something they might live up to: "Like his name, so is he." That saying is found in Scripture, spoken by a woman named Abigail about her husband, Nabal, whose name means "Fool." (I wonder how many wives think their husbands should have been named Nabal!) Nabal had badly mishandled a situation with David's men, and David's army was about to show him who was boss. His wife, in an attempt to cover over her husband's foolish tracks and save his life, told David, "He acts out the meaning of his name: Nabal, Fool. Foolishness oozes from him" (1 Samuel 25:25 MSG). Ouch! And I thought "Mittens" was bad!

Jacob is another guy in the Old Testament whose name foreshadowed a recurring theme that would define a large portion of his life. The name Jacob means "deceiver," and that's a name he lived up to throughout his life, starting with the way he tricked his brother, Esau, out of his birthright (thus entitling him to a double portion of the family inheritance). In and out of conflict his entire life, his deceiving ways led him to a wrestling match with God. Not a metaphorical wrestling match like someone might wrestle with his or her thoughts. This was a physical wrestling match with God that lasted all night, and Jacob fared much better than he could ever have imagined . . . for a while. God "wrestled with him until daybreak. When the man saw that he couldn't get the best of Jacob as they wrestled, he deliberately threw Jacob's hip out of joint" (Genesis 32:25 MSG). Jacob was stubborn in his deceptive ways.

Now, do you think God really needed all night to defeat Jacob in a wrestling match? Jacob would have been in a holy headlock shouting, "Uncle!" in no time if God had wanted it that way. But as is the case for our own struggles in life, this wrestling match wasn't for God—it was for Jacob. After Jacob still wouldn't give in, the Almighty reminded Jacob that he was going toe to toe with, well, *the* Almighty, leaving Jacob in what must have been excruciating pain on the ground with a hip out of joint. But even after this, Jacob continued to hold on to the man. In fact, he told God he wouldn't let go until he promised to bless him. God asked him, "What's your name?" He answered, "Jacob." Just as God didn't need to wrestle with Jacob, he also didn't need to be reminded of Jacob's name. God already knew. So why did he ask? God wanted Jacob to acknowledge who he was and what he was. God was saying, "Jacob, you've lived up to your name, but now own up to it." This is the defining moment toward healing and forgiveness. See, God was about to change Jacob's name and set his feet on a new path.

What if you were named after your biggest character flaw? What would it be? Hello, my name is "Greed"? "Lust"? "Gluttony"? "Pride"? "Liar"? "Selfish"? Jacob isn't the only one who would rather wrestle with God all night before openly examining and confessing his faults or false identities. If you're like me, you quickly thought of an answer to that question I just posed, and it scared you. The journey that leads us to the core of who we really are requires a level of honesty that is uncomfortable . . . about as uncomfortable as a hip knocked out of joint. God knows we were made for more, and we all long to be identified by more than our weaknesses, failures, or faults.

Standing between who you are now and who God is calling you to be is the same question God asked Jacob: "What's your name?" He's asking you, "Are you willing to take an honest, even uncomfortable, look in the mirror and acknowledge who you believe you are?" Most would rather choose to wrestle and wrestle and wrestle with God than face that honest self-examination.

"I don't have a problem with drinking. It's under control."

"Just because I'm flirting doesn't mean I'm going to have an affair."

"I'm not a cutter. I just did it a few times."

"Everybody looks at Internet pornography. I don't have a problem."

Pastor Jim Cymbala wrote in his book *Fresh Wind, Fresh Fire*, "The first step in any spiritual awakening is demolition. We cannot make headway in seeking God without first tearing down the accumulated junk in our souls." I have found that either we are brave enough to pick up the sledge hammer and begin the teardown, or life will do it for us. Like Jacob, how long we wrestle is up to us. God isn't asking you to take that look in the mirror just so he can make you feel worse about yourself than you already do. Everything he calls us to do is out of his great love for us. When we are willing for the "demolition" to begin, the bricks that once formed a wall around our souls are repurposed to build a bridge. A bridge from who we are to who God wants us to become.

"BUT NO LONGER"

Jacob may have lived up to his old name, but God now desired to give him a new one. After Jacob owned up to who and what he was, God said to him, "But no longer. Your name is no longer Jacob. From now on it's Israel (God-Wrestler); you've wrestled with God and you've come through" (Genesis 32:28 MSG). I love that! God, the giver of all names, possesses the authority to decide when you've outgrown one. He crosses out old names and proclaims, "That's not you anymore!" The Bible promises that "you will be given a new name by the LORD's own mouth" (Isaiah 62:2). After all, Paul reminds us that God has started something good in us, but he's far from being finished. "And I am certain that God, who began a good work within you, will continue his work until it is finally finished on the day when Christ Jesus returns" (Philippians 1:6).

I recently visited a women's shelter that my family has supported over the years. While taking a tour of some of their new facilities, my eyes stumbled upon a piece of art on display that was made collectively by women who had walked through the doors of this ministry. They were asked to write down names that they had identified with or had been called in their life that they no longer wanted to carry around. I moved in closer to read what the women had written. I saw names like "Whore," "Unworthy," "Fat," "Stupid," "Meth Head," "Slut," "Good for Nothing," "Baby Killer," "Mistake." The names had each been scribbled on small sticks, and then the sticks were pieced together. The brave women who dared to write down their old names didn't know what the finished art would look like. But the artist did. Once all of the sticks had been collected, the artist masterfully put them together in the shape of a cross. I looked at the cross in a new way that day. I saw painful names, wounded names, guilty names, defeated names, names that no one would be proud to carry. Yet there they were, being carried by a cross. A cross that says, "That may be who you were, but no longer."

HELLO, MY NAME IS
"NEW CREATION"

The decision to surrender your life to Christ is only the beginning of your journey down a long road toward a healthy life and healthy identity. Scripture says God has "begun a good work" in us, but nowhere does it say that the work will be completed this side of eternity. I sure wish it did! We have been promised "that anyone who belongs to Christ has become a new person. The old life is gone; a new life has begun!" (2 Corinthians 5:17). There it is again, the reminder that we are not a finished product. It's only the beginning. I've heard the saying, "The journey of a thousand miles begins with one step." So it goes with the journey of discovering our God-given and God-intended identity.

When we make the choice to step off of the path that leads to sin's destruction, we go under construction. I think of the highway construction in Chicago, where I grew up. It seemed that it took ten years to fix one pothole. And just about the time they finished one project, construction began on another. Likewise, God is continually working on us moment by moment, day by day. But although we are continually under construction, isn't it a relief to know that we don't have to earn or wait to acquire the name "New Creation"? There is no trial period, no checklist to be completed. The moment we stop wrestling like Jacob and believe that our old names have been nailed to a cross, that's it. We immediately receive a new name.

But what happens when you don't feel like a new creation? Or when a new creation gets hit with a wave of old guilt? What happens when our "under construction" state gets discouraging or hits delays? There are many days when I wake up feeling more like an old sinner than a new creation, that's for sure. Henri Nouwen writes in *Life of the Beloved*, "The truth, even though

I cannot feel it right now, is that I am the chosen child of God, precious in God's eyes, called the Beloved from all eternity, and held safe in an everlasting embrace . . . Yes, we must dare to opt consciously for our chosenness and not allow our emotions, feelings, or passions to seduce us into self-rejection." Your status as a new creation is not conditional. It is a firm foundation that cannot be shaken. You will make mistakes, because "all have sinned and fall short of the glory of God" (Romans 3:23 ESV), but once God gives you a name—your true identity—it cannot be taken away.

I love how Scripture tells us that God has the power to literally forget our sins. "I will forgive their wickedness, and I will never again remember their sins" (Hebrews 8:12). I just wish I had that same power. What about you? Do random moments in your day flash back to sins from your past, even down to the littlest of details? Guilt always tries to creep back in, causing you to question something that you confessed and surrendered to God long ago. And Satan loves to use these moments to lie to your heart, trying to convince you that because of your sins, you have lost your God-given title.

These are the times when you must, as Nouwen said, "opt consciously" to believe you are still the new creation God says you are and to be thankful for new beginnings that come with the rising sun each day. "The faithful love of the LORD never ends! His mercies never cease. Great is his faithfulness; his mercies begin afresh each morning" (Lamentations 3:22–23).

What a promise! Fresh mercy today. Fresh mercy tomorrow. Fresh mercy ten years from now . . . and all the way to eternity!

Let the fresh mercy of God refresh your memory every day that although you might have a long way to go in becoming all God created you to be, you are a new creation right here and now. The old has gone and the new has come.

If you were named after your biggest character flaw, what would it be? Why do we allow names like "Greed," "Lust," "Gluttony," "Pride," and others define us?

What's standing between who you are now and who God is calling you to be?

Read Lamentations 3:22–23. How have you experienced God's new (or fresh) mercies day after day? How can you keep believing that they'll never run out?

CHAPTER 13

NOT ENOUGH COOKS
IN THE KITCHEN

I read recipes the same way I read science fiction.
I get to the end and say to myself,
"Well, that's not going to happen."

RITA RUDNER

I love cooking shows. There's just something about watching an expert chef create a culinary masterpiece that I find fascinating. If I'm not careful, I can sit in front of the television totally mesmerized by the Food Network, unable to change the channel while growing increasingly hungry with every dish the celebrity chef puts on display. The funny thing is, no matter how many cooking programs I watch, I have absolutely no desire to do any cooking myself. The chef could be teaching me through the television how to pan sear scallops, but I would have no intention of making my way to the seafood market, let alone firing up a stovetop. I did try to cook our Thanksgiving turkey all by myself once. Emphasis on the word *once*.

Someone had given me this high-tech meat thermometer as a gift. Foolproof, right? I mean, who could screw up a turkey with a device actually telling you when it's done? What I didn't realize was that the meat thermometer, made primarily of plastic, was not designed to remain *in* the oven with the turkey the entire time. When I pulled the turkey out to check its temperature, I found a melted glob of thermometer all over that poor bird. Aside from that one holiday mishap, I've resigned to leave the cooking up to the experts and stay out of the kitchen as much as possible. At my greatest height of motivation, I occasionally think to myself, *I need to try that one of these days*, as I sit on the couch eating Pringles.

How many of us do the same thing with our lives? It's scary how easy it is to watch the hours and days go by and never really engage in the world around us. It's the times that you have said to yourself, *I need to take my wife on a date*, but you never schedule anything. Or *I need to spend more time with my children*, but you never set aside the time. Or *I really need to get out of this job and pursue my real passion*, but you never get around to it. *I should visit my mom*, or *I really need to get plugged in to a small group at church*, or . . . You get the idea. Call it laziness, lack of motivation, fear, whatever. The end result is called missing out. Missing out on that deeper connection with your spouse. Missing out on the reward of your children knowing they matter enough to you that you would carve out extra time for them. Missing out on meaningful relationships, impactful ministry, and spiritual growth. Missing out on discovering your true calling in life. Jesus said, "I have come that they may have life, and have it to the full" (John 10:10 NIV). But many times I live as if my response to Him is, "Hey, Jesus, thanks so much for the offer, but I'll take a rain check."

HELLO, MY NAME IS "UNQUALIFIED"

For some reason, the offer of *life to the full* feels more like a frightening proposition than an exciting invitation. There's something about God's call to something bigger that forces our focus inward. When we feel God inviting us into something greater, we tend to make the mistake of beginning to search ourselves. That search within might be in the hopes of discovering our self-sufficiency, but instead it leads to the discouraging awareness of our own limitations. *I'm too old. I'm too young. I'm too weak. I'm not smart enough. I'm the wrong one for the job. I'm too flawed. I'm unqualified.* But God doesn't call us to things we are capable of accomplishing on our own. Of course, he has gifted each of us in unique ways. We all have different skills, abilities, personalities, and strengths. But God somehow takes all of our good stuff and crafts an original, one-of-a-kind mission for our lives that puts to use everything he's equipped us with and yet still requires something more. That something more is him. His miracle-working power, his strength, his knowledge, his protection, his grace. These God-sized dreams are bigger than the very best you have to offer. Scripture is filled with stories of the greatness people discovered when they bought into their God-sized dream, daring to see beyond their own limitations and trust that God would make the impossible possible.

Moses wanted nothing to do with his God-sized mission. God called him to lead the complaining Israelites out of captivity and into the promised land, but all Moses could think about was all of the reasons he was unqualified for the calling. "Moses pleaded with the LORD, 'O Lord, I'm not very good with words. I never have been, and I'm not now, even though you have spoken to me. I get tongue-tied, and my words get tangled'" (Exodus 4:10). Apparently Moses was no smooth talker. It's funny how we Christians flock to the most eloquent preachers who turn clever phrases and tickle our ears with poetic takes on Scripture. Yet God wanted to use the guy who stuttered. That part of the story alone should encourage you and me to know that he not only will use us in spite of our limitations, but he very well might call us specifically *because* of our shortcomings. The very parts of our lives that we might be tempted to believe disqualify us from a God-sized mission might be the very reason he calls us in the first place.

The Lord challenged Moses to stop looking within and start looking up: "Who makes a person's mouth? Who decides whether people speak or do not speak, hear or do not hear, see or do not see? Is it not I, the LORD? Now go! I will be with you as you speak, and I will instruct you in what to say" (vv. 10–12). Pretty convincing argument from the Almighty. But Moses's awareness of his own limitations and the insecurity he felt about his inability to speak were not going down without a fight. Moses again pleaded, "Lord, please! Send anyone else" (v. 13). Have you ever pleaded with God like that? I know I have.

Not long ago, I was invited to perform a concert in an unlikely place. I've played shows pretty much everywhere. Coffee shops, college campuses, church youth groups, festivals, arenas, you name it. I had developed a confidence that there was nothing that could be thrown at me that could throw me off my game. But just when I thought I had stepped onto every kind of stage there was, God called me to perform inside the walls of a maximum-security prison. I remember trying to find a way out. *God, you've got the wrong guy here. My music won't connect. I won't be able to relate to the inmates. I'm scared.* But the ministry that invited me was persistent, and so I reluctantly agreed to go.

I'll never forget the first steps inside the prison that morning. Surrounded by concrete, barbed wire, and steel bars, it became quite apparent that this would be a concert like no other. The prison chaplain was the first one to greet me. "I'm so glad you could be here today, and I've got some great news for you! I spoke to the prison warden this morning, and he has agreed to allow you to sing in a part of the prison where they never allow any visitors." At that point, I peed my pants. What part of the prison was he referring to, and why would he think I would want to go there? I was about to find out. The guards led me into the solitary-confinement unit that morning. I thought I had seen it all, but this was the first concert venue where I could not even see the faces of my audience. This section of the prison was reserved for the baddest of the bad. The cells weren't like the low-security county jail cells I'd seen on reruns of *The Andy*

Griffith Show. These were more like doors seen on MSNBC's *Lockup*, each with a tiny window and a small sliding door section where food could be passed through without the inmate having contact with the guards.

With my heart pounding and hands sweating, the prison guard stood up to introduce me. Now, I've grown accustomed to some rousing introductions that bring crowds to their feet and excitement buzzing throughout concert halls. This was not like that. Not even close. The guard stepped forward and shouted in a voice that made me want to confess to every bad thing I had ever done, "Listen up! There's a guy here, and he's going to sing. I don't care if you listen or not, but if you make any noise, so help me God, there will be consequences!" I peed my pants a second time. As he finished his introduction, he turned toward me and said with a grin, "Good luck, kid."

Now, I've written hundreds of songs in my career, but surrounded by concrete and steel in that solitary-confinement unit, I could not remember the words to a single lyric I had ever composed. I felt like a stuttering Moses, and I wanted out of there as quickly as possible! I found myself praying, while the silence in the solitary-confinement unit grew increasingly awkward. "God, you better show up right now, because you led me into this mess and I GOT NOTHING!" God answered my prayer and put the words to one song back in my memory that very moment (it was a short concert). I closed my eyes and began singing a song I had written years before called "Only Grace." As I continued singing, I slowly grew the courage to open my eyes. As I did, I began to see the faces of my audience for the first time, appearing one by one in the small windows of each cell door. As I looked out at the inmates staring back at me, it felt as though God was tapping me on the shoulder and telling me, *Matthew, you finally admitted the truth. Apart from me you've got nothing. But look what happens when you take my hand and trust me. I will do all the rest. My grace is sufficient, and I will use you in ways you never imagined.*

I have come to realize that's probably one of God's favorite prayers to hear from his children. "Help! I got nothing!" Jesus tells us that "apart from me you can do nothing" (John 15:5 NIV). I guess when we admit it, that's the best place for the Lord's bigger work to begin in our lives and in the lives of those he leads us to impact. Then, just as I had felt following that prison experience, we are humbled to realize that we were just part of a miracle that was bigger than us. We look back shaking our heads in amazement, understanding what Jesus meant when he said, "Humanly speaking, it is impossible. But with God everything is possible" (Matthew 19:26).

RECKLESS OBEDIENCE

So, if it's all right to admit we've got "nothing," then what *are* the necessary qualifications required to be part of a God-sized plan? The lives of Jesus's disciples have helped me answer that question. Jesus followed in his father's footsteps, calling ordinary people to be part of an extraordinary mission. He overlooked the religious leaders of the day who, on paper, would have been the most qualified to aid in his mission. But a great resume is never what Jesus is looking for—he's looking for a heart that is willing to follow. Jesus called his first disciples, Peter and Andrew, with a simple invitation, "Come follow me . . . and I will send you out to fish for people" (Matthew 4:19 NIV). The disciples' response was not a delayed one. "At once they left their nets and followed him" (v. 20). They didn't respond by saying, "Wow, thanks, Jesus, but . . . uh, can we get back to you on that?" They dropped their nets and lives as they knew them and joined a God-sized mission. James and John did the same. The Bible says they "immediately" followed him.

Why would Scripture bother to describe the speed with which these disciples responded? Perhaps this is so we could see what Jesus is looking for in us. Reckless obedience. Reckless obedience is the result of total trust. If I trust that God's plan is best for me and that he will be faithful to do what he says he will do, then there's no time for doubting my own abilities or lack of preparedness. Like the disciples, he wants our response to be, "Yes, Lord, I'll follow where you lead." I wish I could say that I am just as quick as the disciples were to lay aside fear of my own limitations and follow where God is leading. My reluctant visit to the prison did something to me, though. I may not have been "recklessly obedient," dropping my nets and running straight toward the prison when God called me to go there. But I did eventually obey, and God showed up in a powerful way inside those prison walls. With every step of faith we take, we see the road rise up to meet our feet. And when we experience something special that God is doing, we want more of it. I am getting closer and closer to learning what it means to be recklessly obedient to God on a daily basis, regardless of my doubts in my own abilities or the circumstances around me. I'm learning to step forward and trust that the road will rise up. When I'm on the road he has called me to, I know it always will.

In addition to reckless obedience, Peter and John displayed another key ingredient we need if we hope to be used by God in ways that are bigger than our abilities. In the book of Acts, Peter and John healed a crippled man and were arrested and thrown in jail for preaching about Christ's resurrection. When questioned, they did not cower. They spoke boldly, clearly, and filled with the power of the Holy Spirit, saying, "There is salvation in no one else! God has given no other name under heaven by which we must be saved." Scripture says, "The members of the council were amazed when they saw the boldness of Peter and John, for they could see that they were ordinary men with no special training . . . They also recognized them as men who had been with Jesus" (Acts 4:12–13). I love this description of these two disciples. These guys were as ordinary as they come. No Ivy League education. No special talents. No impressive resume that would command respect, attention, or admiration from anyone. The one thing they had going for them? These men *had been with Jesus*! That was the only explanation for the miracles they were performing and the powerful preaching they were passionately delivering to the people.

When people spend time in *your* presence, can they tell that you've spent time in *his* presence? Peter and John had walked with Jesus, and it showed. Their power came not from themselves, but from being plugged into the ultimate power source. Perhaps you know the feeling of being in the presence of someone who has "been with Jesus." You can tell when you're in the presence of a prayer warrior. I know it when I'm with Matt, the campus pastor at a college in Arkansas. His passion for seeing revival in the lives of college students is contagious. I know it when I'm with Jason, a children's minister in Idaho. He is always asking how he can be praying for me. I know it when I'm with Clark, a graphic designer. His heart for adoption has resulted in two additions to his family. I know it when I'm with Nick, an evangelist who exudes a Christ-like desire to see a lost world find hope. And I knew it when I sat in Billy Graham's kitchen in the mountains of North Carolina and drank root beer with the greatest evangelist of our time. In response to me asking him for advice he said, "Matthew, the success of your ministry, your family, and your entire life all hinges on the success of your time spent with the Lord." That advice has been ringing in my ears ever since that conversation. Each of those people spur me on to reckless obedience and a relentless pursuit of God's presence every day.

FIND YOUR MAC AND CHEESE

Don't laugh, but I have decided to follow my own advice. I'm turning the Food Network off and putting an apron on. See, a show called "Worst Cooks in America" has got me thinking, *How bad can I be?* This show handpicks the people who don't know ketchup from mustard or a fork from a spoon. (One contestant loved vanilla so much that she actually concocted a vanilla chicken recipe. She was vehemently chastised for it, and not allowed to touch the bottle of vanilla again.) I figured, hey, if these people can embarrass themselves on national television, maybe I could at least give it a shot. So I started with baby steps. I found a recipe for a gourmet macaroni and cheese dish that Ina Garten, otherwise known as the "Barefoot Contessa," highly recommended. You should have seen the startled, shocked, and probably fearful looks on the faces of my wife and daughters when I announced that I would be cooking our family's Christmas Eve dinner. And guess what? It was edible! Not only that, but my kids have requested that I make my signature (and only) dish every Christmas Eve from here on out.

God has great plans for you. Plans that will exceed your abilities and qualifications. His plans are so epic that no one would dare think you or I could possibly carry them out in our own strength or power. Satan wants you to focus on what you lack, the skills or gifts you don't possess. He doesn't want you to pick up an apron and step into the kitchen. He wants to make you feel like a nobody who is incapable of doing anything close to great for the kingdom. But read Paul's encouragement here:

> Take a good look, friends, at who you were when you got called into this life. I don't see many of "the brightest and the best" among you, not many influential, not many from high-society families. Isn't it obvious that God deliberately chose men and women that the culture overlooks and exploits and abuses, chose these "nobodies" to expose the hollow pretensions of the "somebodies"? That makes it quite clear that none of you can get by with blowing your own horn before God.

Everything that we have—right thinking and right living, a clean slate and a fresh start—comes from God by way of Jesus Christ. (1 Corinthians 1:27–29 MSG)

Just as he handpicked his disciples, Jesus is still looking for willing hearts who recklessly obey and stay close to his heart. Calling all nobodies, it's time to do great things.

How are you living life to the fullest? Or how are you watching the world just pass you by?

When people are in *your* presence, how can they tell that you've spent time in *God's* presence? How do they see that your power comes not from you but by being plugged into the ultimate power source?

Read 1 Corinthians 1:27–29. How motivated are you to live out God's plan for your life, knowing that you are most likely unqualified and unable to achieve it without him?

CHAPTER 14

86,400 SECONDS

Moses spent forty years in the king's palace thinking
that he was somebody; then he lived forty years in the wilderness
finding out that without God he was a nobody;
finally he spent forty more years discovering
how a nobody with God can be a somebody.
DWIGHT L. MOODY

I have seen the inside of a Waffle House at 3:00 a.m. and lived to tell about it. I was not there because of late-night hunger. (I did eat a waffle before I left, though. Their waffles are delicious!) Strangely, I was there for publicity. I was releasing a new record titled *Live Forever*. One of my inspirations for the record was the number 86,400. That's how many seconds are in twenty-four hours. How do I know that? I googled it. The main theme of this particular collection of songs I was about to release was an encouragement to make the most of the seconds, minutes, hours, and days we are given on earth.

86,400 seconds make 'em count,
make 'em matter,
make your now live forever

Now, sometimes I have a good idea. This was not one of those times. I thought it would be fun to illustrate the message of *Live Forever* by performing twenty-four concerts in twenty-four hours on the day the record was released nationwide. So, my team and I mapped out the different performance locations in and around Nashville. I grabbed my guitar and we gassed up the tour bus for a long night (and morning). I sang the national anthem at a college baseball game. I showed up at Barnes & Noble bookstore and played some tunes. I serenaded travelers at the airport baggage claim #2 while they waited for their luggage. And yes, in the wee hours of the morning, I brought my guitar into the Waffle House just off of I-40 West in an effort to inch closer to the goal of twenty-four performances.

My Waffle House show was far from the largest audience I've ever performed for. But what they lacked in numbers, they more than made up for with their lack of interest. There were three people there: a waitress, a line cook, and a guy in a corner booth who looked as if he wanted to hurt me. But I didn't let that stop me. I picked up my guitar and started strumming. The first song I sang was "Hello, My Name Is." As I belted out the first verse of the song, I was thinking to myself, *This is the dumbest thing I've ever done.* But as I began to sing the chorus, the craziest thing happened! The line cook starting singing along with me as he flipped hash browns and poured the waffle mix.

My solo performance turned into an unlikely duet as we both proudly proclaimed to the rest of Waffle House that we were children of the "one true King."

When we finished singing, the cook smiled at me as he slid across the counter a plate holding a golden-brown waffle and said, "I know that song."

I asked him, "Do you know what that song means?"

His grin widened as he turned back to flip the hash browns on the griddle. "It means I'm blessed and highly favored!"

Over a cold cup of coffee and a butter-soaked waffle, I heard the story of a young man who had overcome many odds just to be where his is now. One might be tempted to look down on a line cook working at a Waffle House at 3:00 a.m., or at the very least feel sorry for him. Working a third shift for minimum wage isn't exactly where most people hope their ladder of success will lead them. But to hear him talk, you'd think he was the richest guy in town. He radiated with a joy, contentment, and gratitude I never expected to find in that dingy little diner. He told me, "All I'm trying to do is show people God's love wherever I go, even in this restaurant." He succeeded that night with me. I shook his hand, left a tip on the counter, and drove off to the next performance of the night, but for the rest of my twenty-four-hour journey I began to rethink what it might look like to be "blessed and highly favored."

BEER AND LIES

I saw a beer commercial that depicted a group of young, attractive people having a poolside party. The men had six-pack stomachs and bulging biceps. The women sported perfect tans and skimpy bikinis. The music was loud and sounded something like Bob Marley would have written. Everyone was dancing, laughing, smiling. This was clearly the party of the century. Just as the scene was set, a celebrity voice-over issued this appealing invitation: "Make this weekend live forever." The message was: *this* is the good life. This party and this drink will give you the kind of experience that will live in infamy, far beyond this weekend.

So many messages the world sends these days sound and look so good, just like that commercial, but they are filled with empty promises. Messages like YOLO (you only live once) tickle the ears of our culture, tempting us to believe that the life we see is all we get. A hit song by everyone's favorite boy band, One Direction, issued this encouragement to millions of their crazed pre-teen fans: "Tonight let's get some, and live while we're young." Messages like that are sending so many of us in the *wrong* direction. YOLO sounds good, but it is a half-truth. And a half-truth is really just a whole lie. It's true that you do only live once, but there is a way to make your life last longer than the here-and-now, and it's not by drinking a certain drink or having a certain kind of party.

In our quest to make the most of the time we have been given in this life, we get lulled into forgetting we were made for more than only *this* life. Scripture says, "He has planted eternity in the human heart" (Ecclesiastes 3:11). Deep inside your heart is a longing for something more than what this temporary life offers. The road between here and eternity has a way of lowering our sights. And when this life matters more than eternity, our goal becomes finding an identity that confirms our success to the world.

I have a friend who felt a stirring to make the most of his time in a more meaningful way. With a hugely successful career in the business world, anyone would look at Lee's life and say he was the American dream personified. Yet what he found at the top of his ladder of success left him feeling discontent. He told me, "The corporate world is all about the here-and-now. The emphasis is on building your kingdom here on earth." Here was a man who had climbed his ladder and reached the top rung. He wants for nothing. No purchase he couldn't afford. Nothing he has yet to accomplish. But at the top of the ladder of earthly success, he looked around only to find that something was still missing. He said something that struck me in a profound way. "I'm tired of living for now. I want to live forever." I wonder if you have ever felt the same way. Maybe you are climbing a different ladder, but yours, too, has left you feeling unfulfilled and with a nagging notion that there is a more significant way to spend the 86,400 seconds God gives you each day.

Some identities we acquire throughout our lives are ones that we are actually proud to display on our nametags. Some sound good and exemplify what success might look like in the world's eyes. Hello, my name is . . . "Popular," "Independent," "Successful," "Respected." Many times our intentions are good, just as Lee's were. He wanted to have a successful career so that he could better provide for his family. So he picked up some nametags that held good titles. Hello, my name is "Successful." Hello, my name is "CEO." Hello, my name is "Wealthy."

You might be proud of the name "Mom," because your world revolves around your kids, whom you love very much. You might have found your identity in a particular relationship or even your marriage. The good names on our nametags, though, don't capture our true identities any more than the negative ones we struggle with. Actually, they can be equally effective in derailing our search to find out who we really are. Our problem is that we so desperately want to find an identity that we pick up any name that feels good and run with it. But both good and bad names in the world's eye can keep us from owning a Christ-centered identity that will make a positive impact on every single dimension of our lives.

- Because I am a child of God, I love being a parent to my children.
- Because I know who I am in Christ, I am able to place my spouse's needs before my own.
- Because I have been bought by a price, I understand that everything I own belongs to God.
- Because God's love for me is not based on my performance, I believe that I am a success regardless of my job title.
- Because heaven is my promised eternity, I know the pleasures of this temporary world won't compare to what's coming.

HELLO, MY NAME IS
"RICH YOUNG RULER"

The guy had everything going for him. The Bible describes him as a "Rich Young Ruler" (Matthew 19 NKJV). How else would one hope to be described? This guy was the epitome of "blessed and highly favored." He had wealth, youth, and power. Yet there he was, coming to Jesus to ask a question that indicated all he had wasn't enough. "Good Teacher, what good thing shall I do that I may have eternal life?" His question proves that eternity has been planted in our hearts and that no matter how many good things we've got going for us, we cannot satisfy the deeper "eternity" void with temporary names. Jesus responded to his question by telling him to "keep the commandments." "Which ones?" the ruler's replied, indicating what he feared letting go of.

This young man wanted eternal life but was trying to figure out what was the bare minimum he had to do in order to live forever. He obviously loved his status in life and was hopeful that he could gain eternal life while not interrupting the good things (or name) he had going for him. Jesus reminded him of the commandments and the man replied, "All these things I have kept from my youth. What do I still lack?" He obviously was feeling pretty good about himself, thinking he was on easy street all the way to heaven. But Jesus knew this man's heart, and with his next instruction pinpointed the one thing that would be hardest for him to part with. "If you want to be perfect, go, sell what you have and give to the poor, and you will have treasure in heaven; and come, follow Me." At this Scripture says the man went away very sad, for he loved his many possessions and the status that came with them.

Good things get in the way of the great things God has for us. Jesus loved this young ruler enough to reach for the one thing standing between him and eternal life—his possessions. Jesus was offering this man the chance of a lifetime. Just as he invited James, John, and the rest of his disciples, Jesus gave this rich young ruler a chance to "come, follow" him. I wonder if this man might have become the thirteenth disciple had he answered Jesus's request with faith and obedience. Instead, he walked away because the name he had made for himself was simply too valuable for him to part with. He settled for a good thing and missed the great things his Savior had for him.

I don't want to walk away like the rich young ruler. My prayer has become, "LORD, remind me how brief my time on earth will be. Remind me that my days are numbered—how fleeting my life is" (Psalm 39:4 NIV). I don't want to waste this brief life by allowing "Selfish" to occupy my nametag. I try to live as a servant every day, even though it doesn't come naturally to me and I fail too many times to mention.

Perhaps you're reading this chapter and find yourself discouraged by how you've been spending your 86,400 seconds every day. Or maybe you're thinking about some of the good names you've owned and placed above your identity in Christ. Well, the fact that you're reading this now means God still has some seconds left on your clock. There is still time to make your *now* live forever. It's not too late for a little course correction.

THE FINISH LINE IS *THAT* WAY!

Portland, Maine, is a city that demands a closer look than the view one might find from a hotel window. The moment I landed in this picturesque harbor city, I knew I had some exploring to do. So I dusted off my running shoes for a morning of sightseeing and sweat. The sun was shining, and I soon found myself on a quiet neighborhood street with no traffic. For some reason I decided to run straight down the middle of the road. I don't know, maybe I've seen the movie *Rocky* too many times. As I ran, I imagined local Portlanders joining me on my run one by one. Children jumping off their bicycles and running by my side. Neighbors cheering me on from their front porches. Instead, all was quiet. No cars. No people. Just me, a tourist running down the street. Then I noticed a man off in the distance, walking toward me. As I got closer to him, I could make out little details of his appearance. He was an older gentleman, with a full head of unkempt white hair. He was wearing a white tank top with holes in it, khaki pants spotted with what appeared to be coffee stains, and a gold chain with a cross around his neck. As I approached him, I cautiously veered from the middle of the road to the right side. And just as I passed him, he called out to me.

"Hey there, sonny! Would you be disappointed if I told you something?"

Caught off guard by his question, I stopped running and turned in his direction. "What's that?" I asked.

Then with a big grin on his face, he pointed over his shoulder, in the opposite direction I was running, and yelled with a cackle, "The finish line is *that* way!"

He really cracked himself up with that joke, and I could hear him laughing all the way down the street as I replied, "Very funny, sir."

Nothing like a crazy old man to drop some perspective on you! The rich young ruler had been given a similar wake-up call. So had my friend Lee. In God's pursuit of us, he wants to redirect our hearts and identities toward the right finish line. We know how the rich young ruler responded. He kept going in the same direction toward the wrong finish line. There is no sadder life story than one who ran the race only to wake up one day and find that the finish line God had intended was clear in the other direction. But my friend Lee? He turned from pursuing corporate success to running toward the stirring in his soul to be a part of something with eternal value. He now serves others like few people I have ever encountered. He is loving big, giving dangerously, and making his *now* live forever.

Charles Spurgeon wrote, "A good character is the best tombstone. Those who loved you and were helped by you will remember you when forget-me-nots have withered. Carve your name on hearts, not on marble." Good character defined by Jesus is found in one who serves, gives, and loves all the way to eternity. When the last of your time on earth has come and gone, it will not matter if your name was on the CEO's office door or a Waffle House cook's nametag. The souls who resist the urge to cling to the mere "good" names this world has to offer are the children of God who know their names will echo for eternity as "blessed and highly favored."

What does it mean to wear the name tag "Blessed and Highly Favored"? And how does that name cause you to live each day and interact with people?

What "good" names by the world's standards have kept you from owning the *great* names God has for you?

Read Psalm 39:4. How much time do you think you have left here on earth? Whether you have months or decades to live, how are you making every second count?

CHAPTER 15

LIFE IS AN AIRPORT

It can hardly be a coincidence that no language on earth
has ever produced the expression,
"As pretty as an airport."
DOUGLAS ADAMS

My flight is delayed. Again. Guess I've come to expect this sort of thing. With all of the traveling I do in a year, I'm actually more surprised when my airplane leaves the runway on time. And don't get me started on lost luggage; that's a whole other chapter. Maybe a whole other book.

Attention passengers for flight #7241 scheduled to leave at 7:50. You didn't actually think we meant 7:50, did you? Silly passengers, we just wanted you all to arrive to the airport early so that we could make you wait. Looks like the joke is on you. Might as well get comfortable, because you're not going anywhere for a while. Have a nice day, and thanks for flying with us.

Okay, maybe those weren't the exact words spoken by the airline employee behind the counter just then. Maybe I'm just a little frustrated. Wouldn't you be? After all, I'm sitting in the Denver airport, which is the last place I want to be. Nothing wrong with Denver, but all I want to do is go home, and I have no say in the matter. Our departure time is up in the air—that's where my plane should be! The plane may have mechanical problems, but I can't fix 'em. They may be short a flight attendant for all I know, but I could never point to all the exits the way they do anyway. Maybe they're running low on fuel, but I couldn't help out there either. Have you seen the price of jet fuel these days?

I guess I've already done all I can do. I arrived at the airport on time. Checked my bags. Stood in line for security check and made it through without sounding the alarms (I almost always forget to empty the change from my pockets). And when I travel with a guitar, the TSA employees always select me for extra screening. They are convinced I'm smuggling drugs or something inside that Gibson. I was patient, though, and let them search until I was cleared for any contraband. Now I'm sitting at the gate, and I guess all that's left for me to do is just wait. Wait to go home . . .

ARE YOU COMING OR GOING?

My unexpected stay in the airport reminds me of the movie *The Terminal* starring Tom Hanks and Catherine Zeta-Jones. On his way to New York City from his homeland of Krakozhia, Viktor Navorski (Hanks) is stopped short of his final destination. En route to the United States, a war breaks out in his home country, which makes his visa invalid upon his arrival. He is a man without a country and is ordered to stay in the terminal of New York's JFK Airport until his status is cleared and visa approved. So Viktor waits, and waits, and waits some more. He winds up *living* in the airport for nine whole months! The closest he gets to the outside world is the view through the glass at the terminal window. Viktor eats in the airport. He sleeps in the airport. He spends twenty-four hours a day in the airport. He even eventually gets a job in the airport. Before long, the airport had become like his home.

One day while Viktor is doing what he always does—wait—he meets a woman, a frustrated flight attendant named Amelia (Zeta-Jones), who in many ways is stuck in her own life. She is involved in a relationship with a married man that she knows is going nowhere, and she has a job that is constantly taking her away from home. Viktor and Amelia become friends and reconnect every time she comes through the terminal on her way to or from a flight. One afternoon over a conversation in the food court, the curious flight attendant asks Viktor, "Are you coming or going?" Viktor, not being quite sure how to respond given his unusual state of stuck-ness, hesitates and then replies, "Both."

I'm trying to picture what that would be like. I mean, what if I find out tonight that my flight is delayed so I begin wandering through the terminal? I notice a newspaper stand and stop in for some light reading. Reading always makes me tense in the shoulders. I notice one of those massage places a couple gates down. A nice chair massage would hit the spot. While

I'm getting my massage, my stomach starts to growl. I wonder what's cookin' in the food court. So I follow my nose until it leads me to some local fare or maybe a Cinnabon (I can smell those things a mile away). Besides, I've got nothing better to do. Hmm, after a good meal, I could go for a little nap. I find a few unoccupied seats all in a row and decide to curl up for a snooze.

Wow, what time is it? Guess I slept a little longer than I expected. I take another stroll around the terminal, and before long I've lost all track of time. You know, I kind of like it here in the airport. Seems like it has just about everything I need. There's even a Starbucks. Hours turn into days and days to months. And before long I can't even remember why I came to the airport in the first place. I forget that I am going somewhere. And when you forget where you're going, you eventually lose the desire to get there.

Sounds pretty crazy, doesn't it? But isn't that how we often live our lives? We get so caught up in the present that we forget about our final destination. We invest everything into this life, as if this life is all we have. But our time on earth is only a brief existence. "As for man, his days are like grass; he flourishes like a flower of the field; for the wind passes over it, and it is gone, and its place knows it no more" (Psalm 103:15–16 ESV). Each life on earth has two things in common: a beginning and an end. And the time in between, our present, is a mere drop of water in the ocean of eternity. As sure as I breathe, I know that one day my lungs will exhale their final breath and I will say goodbye to this life I've built down here. Good thing God's plan for us doesn't end with life on earth. Otherwise, we'd have nothing to look forward to . . . kind of like hanging around the airport with no place to go.

We were made for more than just our present. Beyond the finish line is where our present ends and our future begins. The day will come when all of the children of the King here on earth will be called home to spend eternity in heaven. "My Father's house has many rooms; if that were not so, would I have told you that I am going there to prepare a place for you? And if I go and prepare a place for you, I will come back and take you to be with me that you also may be where I am" (John 14:2–3 NIV). This is God's promise to us: a future in a place far more beautiful and fulfilling than this world could ever be. On the day of Christ's return, we will see our future face-to-face. The reward is not the airport. Not even close.

HELLO, MY NAME IS
"NOT HOME YET"

Troubles at work—how will I provide for my family? Troubles in marriage—how can I save this relationship? Troubles in school—how am I going to get through this semester? Troubles surround us every day. But Jesus never said our days on earth would be trouble-free. Actually, he promised the exact opposite. "In this world you *will* have trouble . . ." (John 16:33 NIV, emphasis mine). Trouble is inevitable. Problems are a part of life. But we all know how easy it is to let the worries of this world overcome our confidence and steal our hope. The English philosopher John Locke put it this way, "What worries you, masters you." While Jesus promised us trouble, in the same verse he also said something to keep our worries from mastering us: "But take heart, because I have overcome the world" (John 16:33). What an awesome message of encouragement for us to hold on to in the midst of this worry-filled airport called life.

There is a purpose for every trial we face and a reward for those whose faith stays strong. First Peter 1:7 says, "These trials will show that your faith is genuine. It is being tested as fire tests and purifies gold—though your faith is far more precious than mere gold. So when your faith remains strong through many trials, it will bring you much praise and glory and honor on the day when Jesus Christ is revealed to the whole world." The trials are preparing us for the day when Jesus comes back.

Some days I find myself longing for heaven more than usual. I turn on the television and catch a few minutes of the morning news, only to be quickly discouraged to see so many people who are hurting. A soldier loses his life. A mother loses her son. A young girl is abducted in a shopping mall. A disgruntled employee goes on a shooting spree. Terrorist attacks. Racial unrest. Politicians arguing. Unemployment skyrocketing. And these are only a few of the morning headlines, a mere glimpse of the vast array of brokenness that surrounds us every single day. Oh, Jesus, you were right. There is trouble in this world.

Beverly has had her share of trouble. But her life didn't start out that way. Married to a great guy named Greg, they had three beautiful, blond-haired daughters, April, Laura, and Kristen. They were a wonderful Christian family, actively involved in the church where I grew up. Greg was an electrician by trade, a board member at the church, and the best volleyball player the church league had ever seen. But at the age of thirty-three, Greg's life faced an unexpected challenge. The picture of perfect health, Greg was diagnosed with lung cancer. He had never smoked a cigarette in his life. Around the same time this family received the devastating news of Greg's illness, they also found out that Beverly was pregnant with their fourth daughter. With trouble circling around this family, our church began to pray and questions began to rise. How could this happen? Why should such an awesome family have to face such a storm? Why is life so unfair? I wish I could tell you that we witnessed Greg's healing on this side of the sky, but only nine months after he was diagnosed, I sang at Greg's funeral. And as I stood in front of the church, trying to make it through the song Beverly had asked me to sing, my eyes were fixed on a pregnant mother with tears rolling down her face and her three little girls looking at their daddy lying in a casket. In that heart-wrenching moment, I mourned for a wife who had to say good-bye to her husband, those beautiful young girls who had to say good-bye to their daddy, and the baby on the way who would never have the chance to know her father.

Have you ever faced a season that begged the question, "Why?" Has there ever been a day when you found your heart crying out, or even praying that God would return quickly to relieve your heart from its brokenness? Maybe like Beverly you've lost a family member or loved one much too soon. When the bad news is more than you can bear, when tears are more frequent than smiles, when pain pushes away the peace, when the questions outnumber the answers, the knowledge that God is with us is all we have to hold on to. "The LORD hears his people when they call to him for help. He rescues them from all their troubles. The LORD is close to the brokenhearted; he rescues those whose spirits are crushed" (Psalms 34:17–18). And we can carry on with the comfort of knowing the immeasurable joy that awaits us in heaven.

Revelation 21:4 tells us, "He will wipe every tear from their eyes, and there will be no more death or sorrow or crying or pain. All these things are gone forever." I like to extend that scripture in my mind sometimes to say, "no more cancer, no more unemployment, no more abuse, no more slavery, no more fighting, no more war," and the list goes on. What wonderful news! What a powerful picture! The hand of heaven reaching out and touching humanity, gently wiping away the tears rolling down our cheeks as if to say, "It's all right now. I've got you."

And although nobody knows the day or hour when Jesus will return and rescue us from the pain in this world (Matthew 24:36), I find peace and comfort in learning a little about God's sense of time. The Creator of the clock has a view of time that is vastly different from ours: "With the Lord one day is as a thousand years, and a thousand years as one day" (2 Peter 3:8 ESV). Knowing that to God a thousand years is like a day kind of brings a smile to my face. That means it could be any day now. And because it could be any day, we must stay faithful and not lose sight of the prize of heaven. "Therefore keep watch, because you do not know on what day your Lord will come" (Matthew 24:42 NIV). You've come this far, so keep holding on because it could be just a few more days. I like what I heard Billy Graham once say. "I've read the last page of the Bible. It's all going to turn out all right."

HELLO, MY NAME IS "GOOD AND FAITHFUL SERVANT"

But how do we make the most of our time on earth as we "keep watch" in the meantime? What exactly does that mean? We cannot just sit around waiting for Jesus to return. There is a purpose in your meantime as well. There is significance waiting to be discovered in your days on earth. Check your pulse. Can you feel that heartbeat? Breathe in deep, and feel your lungs expand. You are alive. But are you fully alive? Are you making the most of this amazing miracle of a life you've been given? Or do you feel like you've just been sitting in the corner of your airport killing time until it's time to go?

Jesus told a powerful parable illustrating what it looks like to make the most of our meantime. A master entrusted his wealth to three of his servants. Two of the servants "put the money to work," doubling the money they had been given by the time the master returned. The other servant dug a hole and buried the money, having nothing but the original amount to show his master when he returned. The master praised each of the servants who made the most of what they had been given by saying, "Well done, good and faithful servant!" (Matthew 25:21 NIV). The main difference between the two servants and the guy who dug a hole? Two of them were faithful. One of them was fearful.

I don't know about you, but I've dug my share of holes in

life. I've buried opportunities that God has given me for fear that it might not go the way I want it to. Fear that I might lose the comfortable life I try to build for myself. Fear that I might be called to risk everything I hold on to so dearly. But I don't want to waste my time digging holes anymore. I want to climb mountains. I don't want to bury the opportunities God gives me to serve him in the ground. I want to reach the end of my life and hear God give me the name "good and faithful servant."

What does it meant to be a good and faithful servant? It means a shift in thinking. It means eyes wide open. It means paying attention to God's leading every moment and every step of the way. It means believing that nothing is insignificant anymore. Every breath you take, every word you speak, every person you come in contact with, even every delayed flight matters. Everything matters because you matter to God. It's what you do while you wait for your final destination that has the chance to echo for eternity.

OUR NAMETAGS WILL
FALL TO THE GROUND

Attention passengers, the time has come. We appreciate your patience. We are ready to board flight #7241 to Nashville. Thank you for flying with us, and we look forward to making you wait in the terminal again soon!

Well, that's my flight. Looks like I'm finally headed home. Suddenly I can see the sky and know that pretty soon I won't be stuck on the ground anymore. I am going home. Viktor got to go home too. He was finally allowed to leave the airport. And even though he made the most of those months in that airport terminal, he was all too happy to head for home. The late Rich Mullins went home sooner than any of his family, friends, or fans expected. Before dying in a tragic automobile accident, the singer/songwriter wrote many songs that clearly expressed his view of this life and his dream for the next. He wrote a line in one of my favorite songs: "No, it will not break my heart to say good-bye." Those words were written by someone who held on loosely to the things of this world because he knew life was only the airport, not the final destination.

Standing in line to finally board my greatly delayed flight, I notice a businessman and beach-bound family reach the line in a hurry at the same time. Earlier in the day, they would have been fighting to be first, but I am surprised to see a smile wash over the businessman's face as he says, "You go ahead. We're all going to the same place anyway." Oh, that we could say the same for every life here on earth. But the truth is, we may not all be going to the same place.

I once read a church sign on the side of a highway that said, "Life has many choices. Eternity has two." My heart breaks when I think of travelers who choose the comforts of this life over the splendor of heaven, not even beginning to comprehend how amazing it will be. "No eye has seen, no ear has heard, and no mind has imagined what God has prepared for those who love him" (1 Corinthians 2:9). I love how Max Lucado describes Christ's return in his book *When Christ Comes*:

The angels bow their heads. The elders remove their crowns. And before you is a figure so consuming that you know, instantly you know: Nothing else matters. Forget stock markets and school reports. Sales meetings and football games. Nothing is newsworthy. All that mattered, matters no more, for Christ has come.

And that is only the beginning! No matter how discouraging your past may have been . . . no matter how difficult your trials may be . . . may you never lose sight of the ultimate goal: an endless eternity in heaven. "Forgetting what is behind and straining toward what is ahead, I press on toward the goal to win the prize for which God has called me heavenward in Christ Jesus" (Philippians 3:13–14 NIV).

The prize is heaven. The prize is eternity. And Jesus promises that everyone who believes in him will receive that prize—everlasting life. The day is coming when all of the nametags we've accumulated, all the false identities we've owned, and all the lies of the enemy we've had a hard time shaking will fall to the ground once and for all as we stand before the Lord. None of it will matter anymore because our true names will be known by him and spoken by him. "All who are victorious will be clothed in white. I will never erase their names from the Book of Life, but I will announce before my Father and his angels that they are mine" (Revelation 3:5). The Bible says we can rejoice to know that our names are "registered in heaven" (Luke 10:20). You're going to stand before Jesus and hear him acknowledge in front of all of heaven, "This one is mine."

Your future is in the making, and it looks good according to what God has promised for all the children of the King. Life is an airport. Heaven is the final destination. And if somewhere along this journey you should be asked, "Are you coming or going?" may you look over your shoulder at the past, look up to heaven and see your future, and with the hopeful heart of a good and faithful servant reply, "Both."

How often do you think of heaven? Describe times when your thoughts turn to eternity.

God promises to wipe away every tear. What events in life have brought you sadness, and what does God's promise to comfort mean to you?

Read the Parable of the Talents (Matthew 25:14–30). What does it look like to be a "good and faithful servant"? And what areas of your life could you change to better reflect your belief that heaven is the real prize?

ACKNOWLEDGMENTS

The process of writing a book can at times feel like the most isolating experience. As if you're stranded on a desert island surrounded by nothing but consonants, vowels, the clicking sounds from your laptop keyboard, and an inner voice saying, "That's no good." One must retreat from the noise and chaos of the world and dare to be alone with one's thoughts long enough to allow that inspiration to take the long journey from the heart to the head to the page. I have found that one of the by-products of this self-imposed solitude is borderline insanity. But just past the insanity is the reward of clarity.

That clarity has brought with it the understanding that I was never really isolated after all. In fact, I had some pretty incredible support throughout this entire *Hello, My Name Is* process, and that means I've got some people to thank!

To my family, you've endured, put up with, suffered through, and politely listened as I read chapters aloud as if practicing for a high school debate, and you have cheered me on the whole time. I couldn't have done this without you.

Steve Green, I'm pretty sure we talk baseball as much as we talk books, and that's just fine with me! Thanks for believing I had this book in me and for navigating the path.

Kyle Olund, the work of editor is something I have a new appreciation for! Thank you for an incredible job done!

Byron, Jeana, Caroline, Nicole, Leeanna, and the entire staff at Worthy—thank you for the opportunity to share my stories with the world.

5by5 Agency, thank you for all your work rallying around what's written in these pages!

Story House Collective, we are building a house on the foundation of the greatest story ever told, and I'm beyond excited to see what God has in store!

Sharen King, you've been a champion. So grateful for your guidance.

To my **popwe** ministry team and board members, thank you for locking arms with me and reminding millions of people that their stories are far from over.

Jordan Jeffers, thank you for telling me your "Hello, My Name Is" story. God continues to use your story in a powerful way to remind us all that there is no more significant title than "Child of the One True King."

ABOUT THE AUTHOR

Matthew West is a four-time GRAMMY® nominee, a multiple-ASCAP Christian Music Songwriter/Artist of the Year winner, Dove Award recipient, and was awarded an American Music Award (2013), a Billboard Music Award (Top Christian Artist, 2014), a K-LOVE Fan Award (2016), and named Billboard's Hot Christian Songwriter of the Year (2016). West also received a Primetime Emmy® Award nomination for Original Music & Lyrics for "The Heart of Christmas" from the film of the same name.

In addition to accolades for his own recordings, West is an accomplished songwriter with more than 130 songwriting credits to his name, including cuts by Rascal Flatts, Scotty McCreery, Casting Crowns, Michael W. Smith, Amy Grant, and Mandisa.

With more than 1.6 million albums sold to date (TEA), he is well known for writing powerful songs inspired by real-life stories. West has received thousands of stories from fans around the world that he regularly revisits and finds inspiration in. His latest album, *Live Forever*, continues that storytelling theme and debuted at #1 on the Billboard Christian Sales Chart. He has achieved record-setting radio success with "Hello, My Name Is" holding the #1 spot for 17 straight weeks, "The Motions" for 15 straight weeks, and most recently with "Grace Wins," his latest song to top the charts.

Also an entrepreneur, in 2016 West launched Story House Collective, a multifaceted brand that will house various media and ministry entities, including his own nonprofit ministry, **popwe**.

FOLLOW MATTHEW WEST ONLINE!

 Matthew West

 @MatthewJWest

 @matthew_west

 MatthewJWest

et Matthew know which chapter was your favorite by posting about it using **#HelloMyNameIs!**

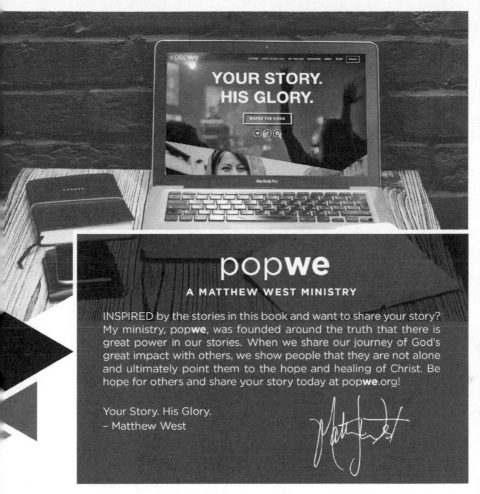

pop**we**

A MATTHEW WEST MINISTRY

INSPIRED by the stories in this book and want to share your story? My ministry, pop**we**, was founded around the truth that there is great power in our stories. When we share our journey of God's great impact with others, we show people that they are not alone and ultimately point them to the hope and healing of Christ. Be hope for others and share your story today at pop**we**.org!

Your Story. His Glory.
– Matthew West

VISIT POP**WE**.ORG TO EXPERIENCE

- An interactive story portal where you can upload a video of your story
- Unlocked Stories from our Vault!
- New CRAFT. SHARE. LIVE. story resources
- Small group and ministry resources
- Volunteer opportunities, including our Concert Prayer Ministry and much, much more!

We're so excited to share our ministry resources with you and hope you will be inspired to CRAFT. SHARE. and LIVE. your story for **HIS GLORY!**

Join pop**we** *Nation!*
Daily Devotions | Resources | Get Involved

IF YOU ENJOYED THIS BOOK, WILL YOU CONSIDER SHARING THE MESSAGE WITH OTHERS?

Mention the book in a blog post or through Facebook, Twitter, Pinterest, or upload a picture through Instagram.

Recommend this book to those in your small group, book club, workplace, and classes.

Head over to facebook.com/matthewwest, "LIKE" the page, and post a comment as to what you enjoyed the most.

Tweet "I recommend reading #HelloMyNameIs by @matthew_west // @worthypub"

Pick up a copy for someone you know who would be challenged and encouraged by this message.

Write a book review online.

Visit us at worthypublishing.com

twitter.com/worthypub

worthypub.tumblr.com

facebook.com/worthypublishing

pinterest.com/worthypub

instagram.com/worthypub

youtube.com/worthypublishing